Praise for

When God Happens

"True stories like these require those who don't believe in angels, or the God who sends them, to explain the unexplainable. A related question: who wants a God one can explain, who would be no God at all?"

—**CAL THOMAS**, syndicated columnist

"These real stories of how God miraculously altered situations for the love of His people are a powerful read."

—**DIMAS SALABERRIOS**, author of *Street God*

"Reading *When God Happens* is like receiving an intravenous dose of hope in a world parched by hopelessness. It will remind you not just to hope for miracles but to expect them."

—**MELANIE HEMRY**, *Guideposts* magazine writer and author of fifty-four books

When God Happens

WHEN

TRUE STORIES OF
MODERN DAY MIRACLES

GOD

ANGELA HUNT AND **BILL MYERS**

HAPPENS

SALEM
BOOKS

Salem Books™ is a trademark of Salem Communications Holding Corporation; Regnery® is a registered trademark of Salem Communications Holding Corporation

Scripture quotations marked (ESV) are from The ESV® Bible (The Holy Bible, English Standard Version®), copyright © 2001 by Crossway, a publishing ministry of Good News Publishers. Used by permission. All rights reserved.

Scripture quotations marked (NLT) are taken from the Holy Bible, New Living Translation, copyright © 1996, 2004, 2007, 2013, 2015 by Tyndale House Foundation. Used by permission of Tyndale House Publishers, Inc., Carol Stream, Illinois 60188. All rights reserved.

Scripture quotations marked (NIV) are taken from the Holy Bible, New International Version®, NIV®. Copyright © 1973, 1978, 1984, 2011 by Biblica, Inc.™ Used by permission of Zondervan. All rights reserved worldwide. www.zondervan.com The "NIV" and "New International Version" are trademarks registered in the United States Patent and Trademark Office by Biblica, Inc.™

Cataloging-in-Publication data on file with the Library of Congress

ISBN 978-1-62157-713-3
e-book ISBN 978-1-62157-714-0

Published in the United States by
Salem Books
An Imprint of Regnery Publishing
A Division of Salem Media Group
300 New Jersey Ave NW
Washington, DC 20001
www.SalemBooks.com

Manufactured in the United States of America

10 9 8 7 6 5 4 3 2 1

Books are available in quantity for promotional or premium use. For information on discounts and terms, please visit our website: www.Regnery.com.

Jesus also did many other things. If they were all written down, I suppose the whole world could not contain the books that would be written.

—*John 21:25, NLT*

contents

INTRODUCTION

R eading and writing about miracles can be a tricky thing.
On the one hand, we don't want to exploit the sensational—turning God's work into a sideshow spectacle, suggesting He's some sort of magician who must perform to convince a skeptical audience of His existence. In fact, it was Jesus who said, "An evil and adulterous generation seeks for a sign" (Matthew 16:4, ESV).

There's also the danger of suggesting those who experience the miraculous hand of God are somehow special or more loved than the rest of us.

Yet by refusing to share and celebrate His miraculous doings today, are we not putting His light under a bowl and refusing to let His love shine to an ever-darkening world?

Our aim in this first volume (of what we hope will be many) is to share His goodness, allowing a starving, yet doubting world to see more of who He is. We want to encourage others with the fact that there are no laws of physics or science a loving God must follow to express His love.

In short, we hope each of these following stories will display a particular aspect of His glory:

- **"Miracle on Highway 6"** describes God breaking the laws of space-time to empower a Good Samaritan couple with the help of two "mysterious strangers" to perform the impossible after a fiery crash
- **"A Season of Angels"** reveals how the terrorist action of blowing up the federal building in Oklahoma City caused a young woman to encounter three very different angels
- **"She Wrote, 'Miracle of God'"** captures how God brought a newborn, who was diagnosed as medically dead, back to life
- **"She Belongs to Him"** shows the great lengths to which God will go in order to protect His chosen from the hands of the enemy
- **"Writing on the Wall"** illustrates that God can use even the classified section to make His will known
- **"Pursued by God"** conveys God's great love for those who persistently pursue Him
- **"When God Heals"** demonstrates that God is interested in healing not only physical bodies but also broken hearts
- **"Supernatural War"** explores the power of Christ working through even the most inexperienced to set a prisoner of Satan free

In Revelation 12, Scripture says we triumph over the enemy with two things:

- The blood of the Lamb
- The word of our testimony

That's what these accounts are: testimonies. They are a reminder that the God who reached down to touch those He loved in Bible days has not changed. He has not turned His back on us or left us to our own devices. As Scripture also states, "[He] is the same yesterday, today, and forever" (Hebrews 13:8, NLT).

Of course, there's always the risk of comparison. We may find ourselves asking, "If God healed *them*, why didn't He heal me?" We wish there was one clear answer. There is not. Sometimes it may be because we are asking for a cheap substitute when He has planned something far greater than we can comprehend. Like little children, we may be asking for a truckload of candy bars when He has a full course (and far healthier) meal just around the corner. Maybe, as a friend, James Watkins, suggests, there are times God insists on giving us bread and fish when in our ignorance we are demanding scorpions and snakes.

With that in mind, maybe it's a good policy to never demand answers from God. "Why are You doing this? Why are You doing that? Why aren't You doing it my way?" There are very few instances in the Bible where God gives an account of His actions. In the best case, it would be like explaining quantum mechanics to your pet. In the worst case, our questions would lead to the gross and dishonoring act of a creation insisting its Creator defend Himself—something that in all of human history has never turned out well. Instead of standing on the railroad tracks to demand an oncoming freight train stop and explain its intentions, it's more profitable to ask God *how*. "How can I use what is happening to accomplish Your purposes? How can I use it to get on board to wherever You're taking me?" And, most importantly, "How can I use this situation to Your glory?"

We have been diligent to confirm the accounts in this volume are true. Many are from authors and friends we trust. We've asked others to verify the facts of stories from those we don't personally know.

Finally, if you have a miracle story that can be verified, and if you think it will encourage others, please drop us a line at www.WhenGodHappens.com.

We trust and pray you'll find these testimonies as inspiring as they were to us.

Angela Hunt
Bill Myers

CHAPTER ONE

MIRACLE ON HIGHWAY 6
CHERI CLEMMONS

On March 25, 2009, I developed a craving for hot dogs. The more I attempted to ignore the craving, the stronger it became. "Cody," I told my husband, "I know we are eating healthy to shed this winter weight, but I really have a hankering for hot dogs."

I was surprised by his response. "Me, too! I didn't want to say anything, but my craving is turning into an obsession. Well, if we're going to cheat on our diets, then let's get a hot dog worth the extra calories. What do you say we have a little cheat meal and enjoy a kosher dog?"

I grinned. "I'd say you're the man with the plan."

We looked forward to our "forbidden" meal, but a powerful thunderstorm moved in and showed no signs of moving out.

"Cody," I said when my stomach began to rumble, "it's six thirty. How much longer do you want to wait out the storm?"

Cody studied the sheets of rain hitting the driveway and flowing into the yard. He let out a deep sigh. "Let's head into town. Maybe the storm won't seem so bad once we're on the road."

We had only traveled a quarter mile when a truck pulled a U-turn in front of us.

"Cody, look out!" I braced myself for impact.

By some miracle, our hydroplaning car avoided hitting anyone else. We stopped on the shoulder a short distance away from an accident. Looking over my shoulder, I saw an SUV upside down in a ditch. Flames appeared near the engine, and a crushed compact car rested next to the SUV.

Instinctively, I reached for my phone and dialed.

"Nine-one-one. What's your emergency?"

"There's been a really serious accident on Highway 6," I said. "We have a vehicle upside down and on fire! These people are trapped and we need the Jaws of Life. We need help *now*!"

Words seemed like pitiful tools to express the urgency of the situation, but a conviction rested at the center of my gut. No one was going to die here today. I would *not* watch anyone die. God was going to show up and save those people.

I bolted from the car as I called my parents. "Mom, you need to start praying! Call your neighbors. There's been a serious accident with one car already on fire."

Screams and frantic cries pierced the early evening air. Making my way to the SUV, I spotted the source of the sounds: two little girls with a man in the tall grass. Later, I learned the man reached through the broken rear window and pulled the girls from the backseat of the vehicle. Their nanny was driving them home from school when the accident happened.

In front of the SUV, a bearded, young man in glasses scooped water from the rain-filled ditch and attempted to douse the flames.

He paused only long enough to acknowledge me then backed away from the car. "Get back! It's going to blow!"

"Is anyone else in the vehicle?"

"I don't know, but you need to get back. It's going to explode."

The man with the two girls echoed the warning. "Get away. It's not safe!"

I looked back at the upside-down SUV. Flames rolled around the driver's window, obscuring my vision. Sprinting around the back, I picked my way between the vehicles and peered into the compact car. The driver's arm hung slightly out the window, and his head sagged forward and to the right. I could see broken glass in his ear and blood on his clothes.

My mind raced. His legs. Where were his legs?

His legs disappeared into the mangled wreckage, and the steering wheel cut into his torso. I knew no one could free him from the wreckage without divine intervention. I took a deep breath, reached out, and squeezed his forearm. I felt a supernatural authority rise within me as I declared, "You are going to be okay."

He lifted his head and looked at me, his eyes bulging from their sockets. He groaned. "—I'm not."

"Yes, you are. God is going to get you out of there."

Now, to check on the other driver—the nanny. I dropped to my hands and knees. Sharp metal and broken glass pressed into my palms as I crawled toward the SUV. My head almost touched the ground as I peered through the driver's window. I locked eyes with a lady hanging upside down. "How many people are in there with you?" I called.

"It's just me." She paused, looked down, and then looked back at me. "My left foot is on fire. But if you have a knife, you can cut me out."

I circled the vehicle and saw fire filling the vehicle. The driver's window went black as flames licked against it.

As Cody raced toward me, I cried, "Cody, get your knife! There's a woman on fire and trapped in her seat belt. She said you can cut her out."

Cody quickly ran to our car and retrieved his knife. I called my parents again, my voice quivering. "Dad, a lady is on fire and trapped in her car. Cody is going to try to climb in and get her out. Pray! Call nine-one-one and tell them we need help now. People are burning."

"Tell me where you are. I'm on my way."

"Dad, there's no time. The fire is spreading, and Cody is going in now."

I could hear fear in my father's voice. Always quick to jump in and help people, Dad had no choice but to trust God this time.

Standing close behind my husband, I watched as he got down on his knees and squeezed between the vehicles. He tugged a solid sheet of cracked glass from the SUV's front window. Mumbling, "I can't fit," he continued to look for a way into the car.

I could hear Cody asking God to help him, to show him what to do. Finally, he squeezed his upper body through a back window. The space allowed him to slide the knife toward the trapped woman.

The vehicles were so tightly jammed together that I had to stand behind Cody and lean over him. "Tell me what to do to help. Tell me what to do to help," I said.

With Cody in the vehicle up to his belly, I caught a glimpse of the woman's hands when the first explosion rocked us. A fireball consumed Cody and the woman, and the shock knocked my head back as the flames rolled over me, wrapped around my bare legs, and skipped up my back. I was aware of the heat but more aware of an odd quiet—my husband had fallen silent.

Memories of a documentary about a submarine explosion ricocheted through my brain. That explosion robbed the sailors of oxygen, suffocating them.

The deafening silence, combined with that awful memory, kicked me into prayer overdrive. I prayed in words and groanings, trusting the Holy Spirit to convey my thoughts and feelings.

I grabbed Cody by the hips and yelled, "Tell me what to do!" An instant later, I heard the most beautiful sound—Cody talking. "Put your hands over your head," he told the trapped woman, "and I'll pull you out."

As the sharp knife cut through the seat belt, the woman dropped from where she was dangling. Then I saw her lock eyes with Cody. She wasn't going to make it out. The driver's headrest was in the way, leaving only a six-inch gap through which she would have to crawl.

Recognizing his task was impossible, Cody cried out to God.

Still gripping Cody, I felt a bump against my hip. From the corner of my eye, I saw a flash of bright, white light, and then smooth porcelain hands reached past me and grabbed Cody and the woman. In the blink of an eye, those two were lying on the grass next to me. I heard the *pssshhhhtt* of a fire extinguisher as someone doused the flames on the woman's lower body.

But Cody wasn't thinking about his close call; he was thinking about the man in the compact car. On his knees, he looked up at me with desperation in his eyes. "If we were in our truck, we could push the burning SUV off the other car."

A lady in the crowd ran over to help Cody move the injured woman away from the fire as I ran over to the smaller vehicle.

My mind raced to come up with a solution. "God send your angels to get this man out of the car. Send them *now*!"

I could feel faith rising in my chest, stirring inside me as my prayers become more fervent.

These were not prayers of desperation that begged and pleaded for God to show up. I prayed ferocious prayers of faith and authority, commanding the angels of the Lord to save the young man.

After several failed attempts to enlist the help of bystanders, I was rushing back to Cody when a large explosion engulfed both vehicles in flames. Horrified, I turned toward the small car. Through the flames, I could make out the shape of a man's head. His neck and shoulders slumped toward the passenger side as thick smoke and flames rolled over him. Cody saw the man, too. His mouth dropped open as shock and horror swept across his face.

With my eyes closed, I belted out from the depth of my soul, "Lord, send your angels now!"

"Cheri—look!" I opened my eyes and followed Cody's pointing finger. The young man was lying in the grass not far from his car. His arms stretched over his head as a weak cry for help escaped his lips.

What? How did he get out of the car? Who put him in the grass?

With no time to wonder about details, I hurried over to the young man and collapsed in the grass next to him. I hesitated to touch him because his condition was not good. When I first saw him in the car, he was covered in blood but not burned. Now his skin was black.

I closed my eyes and prayed. A moment later a warm hand grasped mine, and a woman leaned against me, joining with me in prayer for God's mercy.

I don't know how long we prayed for that young man, who we later learned was named Tony. When I finally opened my eyes, I noticed a stranger sitting at Tony's feet and a slender, gray-haired man kneeling a few inches in front of me. He leaned forward, gazed intently into my eyes, and smiled. "Calm down," he said. "Everything is going to be all right."

I smiled in return, nodding as I continued to pray. The man had a reassuring and gentle voice. And his eyes—they were pools of love. Nothing about that man felt natural to me, not for that time and place.

Several smaller explosions rained debris over us, spurring me to duck and run for cover.

Free of the blinding smoke, I spotted Cody lying in the grass next to the woman from the SUV. Mud, broken glass, and blood stained his clothes. The woman was alive and people were caring for her.

I looked at the lady still holding my hand. "That's my husband over there in the grass. I've got to check on him."

As I approached Cody and the woman from the SUV, I saw the sweetest thing I've ever seen in my life. Smiling while holding the woman's hand, Cody said, "Dear, I think you're going to need a haircut after this."

The woman looked up at Cody with an impossibly wide smile. My heart melted as love and peace washed over me. A short conversation followed introductions. The woman's name was Linda. Cody declared he was fine. A few minutes later, Linda said, "Would you mind calling my boss and letting her know I may be late to work in the morning? And someone ought to call the girls' parents and let them know about the accident."

You could have knocked me over with a feather. Was she kidding? What kind of woman could have burned feet, a crushed hip, a broken leg, scorched hair, and enough of her wits about her to think of those kinds of phone calls? Talk about a dedicated employee!

Emergency responders started preparing the injured for transport to the hospital.

When the lady who was praying with me walked over, I made some introductions. "This is my husband, Cody."

"Oh! This is *your* husband? I helped him pull Linda up the hill. I'm Terri."

"Well, thank you, Terri, for helping Cody pull Linda out of the car."

She shook her head. "I didn't. No one did. No one was with you."

"No, someone bumped into me, and I saw arms reach past me. I assumed they were yours."

She smiled. "No one was with you. Standing on the hill, I watched you and your husband between the cars. Then there was an explosion and you guys were surrounded by flames, so I couldn't see you anymore." More emphatically, she repeated, "No one else was there, only you two."

Could she be right? I glanced back at the wreckage where the two cars lay next to each other. How could more than two people even fit in the space? It was so narrow that I had to stand *behind* Cody.

A paramedic came over to examine Cody. After a cursory look, he told Cody he ought to go to the hospital. "We ran out of supplies, so I can't take care of this here."

A Good Samaritan overheard the conversation and brought alcohol and gauze for Cody's wounds. When a news crew approached for an interview, Cody shook his head. "No, thank you. I don't want to be on the news."

Terri grabbed Cody by the arm. "You have to tell them! There was a miracle on Highway 6 tonight, and angels showed up. I'll tell them with you!"

She was right, of course. At least two angels had been on the scene, maybe more.

I clung to Cody's arm and surveyed the scene around me. The highway was closed in both directions, creating a line of vehicles stretching toward both horizons. A CareFlight helicopter sat in the center of the highway, blades slowly turning as an EMT loaded one of the little girls. The flashing lights of numerous emergency vehicles dotted the landscape.

Then I saw it—a perfect rainbow stretching from horizon to horizon over the scene. The news crew started to film the rainbow as people around me pointed.

Still visibly shaken, Cody gripped my hand. "I could see the vehicle filling with flames, and I could feel the heat on my face. I told God I was scared and didn't want to die this way. I didn't want to be burned up or scarred for life."

I looked at Cody's bloody face and hand. "I have to agree with the paramedics on this one. You really should go to the hospital and get a few stitches."

Cody grinned. "I'm not going to the ER unless I can get a shower and clean clothes first. I'm not sitting in a cold room all night in wet clothes."

When we got home, I stopped Cody before he could shower. "Wait, I have to get a picture of you."

"Like this? What on earth for?"

"I want to get a picture because you have never looked more handsome than you do right this minute."

I snapped the picture and smiled. I didn't want to ever forget the miracle God performed that night. I wanted to pet my husband's face and feel his smooth, unburned skin.

While I waited for Cody to clean up, I absently brushed the front of my jacket. I hesitated when my fingers felt a crusty texture, and I glanced down, expecting to find a layer of mud.

I discovered melted fabric instead.

⁓

We arrived at the hospital amid a buzz of activity. The staff coordinated with other hospitals to send the injured to units best suited to their specific injuries. We asked about Linda and the young man from the compact car, but they could only tell us the victims were taken to other hospitals.

The nurse knew about the accident but wanted to hear details. We recapped the accident, telling her about the fires, angels, and miracles. Her expression slowly changed. She furrowed her brow, cocked her head to one side, and narrowed her eyes. "Your voice wasn't raspy when you got here, and you didn't have a cough. We need to check you in because that's not a good sign. We need to take a look at your lungs."

The doctor entered the examination room, sliding into the chair in front of Cody while flipping open his chart. "I see you have a contusion on each side of your forehead, minor burns on your hands and face, and a couple of gashes we're going to suture. The x-ray also shows something deep in your hand, glass or metal—I can't be sure. I'll try to get it out first. So, tell me about these injuries."

The doctor glanced back and forth between us, listening intently as we tag-teamed our narrative.

As we finished our story, the doctor leaned forward and inspected my jacket. The front, the side, one entire sleeve, and half of the back was melted. Taking a penlight out of his breast pocket, he inspected my nose and ears, looked at my jacket again, and then studied Cody's face. "We have a medical term for this," he said. "It's called a miracle of God, and there is no other explanation. Your husband's face should be more melted than your jacket."

After several failed attempts to locate the object made visible by the x-ray, the doctor said, "The more I dig around in your hand trying to locate this object, the more risk I run of damaging tissue. You need to have an orthopedic surgeon look at this. In the meantime, I'm going stitch you up, and then you'll be good to go."

He looked at me. "You, on the other hand, we'd like to keep for observation tonight. You have smoke and heat damage to your lungs and larynx."

Since we didn't have health insurance, we opted to go home with a stern warning to return immediately if my condition changed.

Well after one o'clock in the morning, we were still excited as we stopped at a twenty-four-hour drugstore. A young man, his hoodie pulled low over his eyes, asked us for change. Cody's heart went out to the boy. After giving him money, Cody asked the young man to come inside with us.

I walked over to the pharmacist to give them privacy, and later Cody told me what happened.

My husband wasted no time sharing the gospel. "Do you know who Jesus is?" he asked.

"Yeah," the young man replied. "Sometimes I go to church with my grandma. That Jesus, He's a good man."

"He *is* a good man. But Jesus is much more than that." Cody explained salvation and why we need a savior. Then he shared details of the accident to point out how fast things can change. "Hell is a real place with real flames," he said. "If an unsaved person were to die today, those flames would be their reality for eternity. I'm telling you things can change fast. You can walk out of here tonight, be shot by a rival gang member, hit by a car, and killed. You don't know what your future holds."

The boy got the message and wanted to accept Christ as his savior. Cody took his hands and led him in prayer. That boy was unashamed and hungry for the love of Christ he felt in Cody. He wanted to know Jesus, the One who can pull people from burning cars and change lives.

⁓

Several days later, we went to the hospital. Through a partially open door, I could see Linda eating lunch, so I stepped into the room. "Linda? Do you know who I am?"

She looked past me at Cody and smiled. "No, but I know *him*. Your face doesn't look familiar, but your voice—I know your voice. I heard you praying."

She recounted the accident with the same calm demeanor I had witnessed days before. Linda said that as soon as Cody cut the seat belt and she fell onto the ceiling, she realized she would burn to death because there was no way out. She asked God to send an angel and then felt a presence in the vehicle with her. She saw Cody's hands reaching for hers. Then a bright light flashed, and another set of hands reached into the vehicle.

As we talked, I realized that in our weakness God shows Himself strong, showing up in a situation where man is helpless to do anything. God created physics, so we shouldn't be amazed or surprised when He bends the laws of science and nature to perform miracles. Yet I am continually awestruck by the God we serve.

⁓

Two weeks later, I was sitting on an examining table, slightly frustrated because I was not healed. I listened as the doctor explained why lungs were slow to mend. "It's difficult to get medication down in them to help the healing process." He picked up his prescription pad and wrote two prescriptions: one for medicine, and one for me *not to talk* for seven days. "I want to see you back again, and we'll discuss speech therapy."

When I squeaked out, "After therapy, will I have a better singing voice?" I got a brief smile followed by a stern look. "No, but you will learn how to talk without stressing your vocal cords. Without undergoing any sort of procedure, we won't know the full extent of damage. You run the risk of forming scar tissue and altering your voice permanently."

On the way to the pharmacy, Cody picked up the second prescription and waved it. "I know a lot of guys who would love to have one of these." He grinned. "Next visit, I'm going to ask if I can get a stack for my friends."

I gave him *the look* and scratched out the following note: Laugh it up, funny boy.

Later I asked God why He was taking so long to work on my lungs. "You miraculously removed whatever was lodged in Cody's hand, and I'm so thankful. You saved people from burning vehicles. I know You can heal me instantly, and I'm not complaining. I just don't understand why it's taking so long."

I felt God respond: "Your physical injuries are the evidence your story is true. Otherwise people would question your testimony." In my mind, I heard His belly laugh. "You know, daughter, next time, just ask. I'm not hard of hearing." I could feel God's love for me, and His pleasure with my zeal. And yes—everything was going to be all right.

On Easter Sunday, we were excited to meet the two little girls who were involved in the accident. Cody also spotted the Good Samaritan who had tended to his hand. We were thankful to be able to properly introduce ourselves and thank the lady for her kindness.

Turning, we saw the little girls who had been on their way to school. One sat in a wheelchair, and the other stood beside it. The accident had left one girl with two broken legs and the other with a concussion.

The girls' parents smiled and asked their daughters, "Do you know who these people are?"

I bent to gaze at their beautiful little faces.

"Yes." The girl in the wheelchair gazed up at Cody. "I recognize him. That's our angel."

Looking back at me, she said, "I don't know your face, but we heard you praying. *Everybody* heard you praying."

I laughed. "Yes, rumor has it that God's not hard of hearing."

People who recognized Cody from the news story often called him a hero, shaking his hand and asking to know more about the accident.

At first Cody was uncomfortable with the attention and the word "hero." He was always quick to tell people, "I'm no hero. I was afraid to burn up or die."

In His perfect mercy and grace, God revealed that courage is not the absence of fear. Courage is facing your fears with faith.

Through our miracle story, God has given us opportunities to pray for people who would not otherwise be open to hearing the gospel. Their perspective of a hero is the hook that draws them in, making them eager to know the God of salvation.

I don't know if we will ever learn everything that happened that day, but God continues to reveal astounding details. A firefighter told us the compact car's steering column pinned Tony to the driver's seat, breaking four of his ribs. "We found the steering column bent and broken away from him, permitting his escape."

I don't know who broke that steering column, but it would have been humanly impossible.

Terri and three other eyewitnesses said angels carried Tony from his car. "He was unconscious, yet his arms were above his body as if someone was carrying him."

The DPS officers had never seen an accident of this magnitude with *no* loss of life. Cody received their Directors Award for the role he played that day.

As we trusted God to pay our medical bills, Cody also received the Carnegie Medal. The cash award covered our expenses.

A fireman told us that the human lung suffers damage at 120 degrees, but the temperature must be much higher for a jacket to melt. Another testament to the miracle of Cody's face not being burned.

During an interview with *The 700 Club*, I learned Tony saw a man sitting in the back seat who matched the description of the angel I saw. The angel smiled at him in the rearview mirror and said, "Calm down. Everything is going to be all right."

Our lives have changed a lot since that day in March 2009 when God supernaturally intervened in a natural world.

On Mother's Day of that same year, Tony accepted Jesus Christ as his Savior.

A few months later, God inspired us to start What If Ministry, which helps people with difficult questions find their answers in God's Word.

In May 2010, my dad went to be with the Lord. The miracle on Highway 6 changed my father's view of God. The realization that God is a loving Father spurred him to surrender his life to Christ.

Our pastor says it best: "Our lives need to be supernaturally natural and naturally supernatural."

Every day I am humbled, and I marvel at what God has us doing as we continue to live out Isaiah 6:8: "Here I am. Send me" (NLT).

Married in 1987, **Cody and Cheri Clemmons** enjoy a life of pursuing God in central Texas. In 1992, they founded Tatonka Cartridge Company, which manufactures shooting sports related gift items. A few months after the miracle on Highway 6, they were asked to conduct church services at a local nursing home. At the same time, God inspired them to start What If Ministry, which helps people with difficult questions find their answers in God's Word.

Cody and Cheri were ordained in 2014. They currently serve on the Council for the Texas Apostolic Prayer Network and on the Intercessory Team for their local church, Christ the King Baptist Church in Waco, Texas.

CHAPTER TWO

A SEASON OF ANGELS
RENE GUTTERIDGE

When I was a little girl, I always worried about heaven. I really enjoyed all that life had to offer me as a creative, energetic, curious child. And I often lay in bed at night, staring at the ceiling, hoping that when I died I wouldn't be bored. My best efforts at imagining what heaven would be like was awfully underwhelming considering I'd one day be a creative writer. In my mind's eye, I only managed to see fluffy clouds strewn across baby blue skies. I imagined myself wandering around those clouds, floating more than walking, but never able to fly, hoping to come across an angel or two for some entertainment in what I was told would be eternity.

Books and movies didn't help my imagination break new ground on this subject. Angels were depicted in white, flowing robes (however did we see them against all those white clouds?), strumming a harp or blowing a trumpet, all the while keeping long blond hair away from their glowing faces.

As I grew older, I bought into the idea that maybe, just maybe, there was one special angel assigned to keep me safe. Which kind of embarrassed me. It felt a little Big Brother-ish. I was thankful for him or her (I never could quite figure out which sex to assign to my angel), but I didn't want the angel all up in my business too much. I remember thinking as a teenager, "Just make sure I don't get hurt and stuff, but don't be a snitch, okay?"

I was kind of bossy, wasn't I?

In my late teens, I was pretty convinced my angel was doing a good job watching over me. I saw some friends die early and realized life was as fragile as all the adults kept telling me it was. By then I was growing in my relationship with God, too, so I'd passed the "fluffy white cloud" phase of heaven. Though I wasn't ready to go on to eternity, I was pretty certain it was going to be cooler than a sky full of cotton balls. But angels—I still didn't quite have a grasp on them. Were they invisible, ghost-like entities walking right past me and through the next wall? Did they have wings? I hadn't a clue.

Starting on the morning of April 19, 1995, my ideas about who angels were and what they did was about to change. I was twenty-two years old and working in part-time ministry for First United Methodist Church in downtown Oklahoma City, Oklahoma. I was supposed to be at work at 9:00 a.m., but I was running late as usual. As I hastily tried to get out my apartment door, the phone rang. It was Mom, asking me to run by her work. She needed me to sign some papers. I explained I couldn't, but she insisted. Something about insurance deadlines. I sighed, hung up the phone, and raced to her office to get those papers signed, still trying to not be late for work.

It was that single phone call, delaying me by no more than five minutes, that saved my life. As I walked out of the building where my mom worked, I remember a man held the door for me. And just as he smiled at me and I stepped out, an enormous BOOM shook the ground and rattled the windows rising far into the sky above us.

"What was that?" he gasped.

"I don't know," I said, looking up.

"Maybe a sonic boom," he said. But then he shook his head. "No. It couldn't be."

We went on about our business. But, just a couple of short miles away, I discovered where the noise came from. As I turned onto the street leading me to work, so did a fire truck, its sirens screaming. It wasn't the only siren reverberating against the brick walls of downtown Oklahoma City. Suddenly the entire city seemed on fire.

As I rounded the corner, I saw black smoke rising hundreds of feet into the air. And the building I always drove past, which was right next to where I worked, was nearly gone. I pulled my car over but left it in the street. I got out and ran a block south to try to get to the church, trying to find the people I worked with.

I spent another eight hours or so downtown. We soon discovered it wasn't an airplane that had crashed into the building, as it first looked. A bomb had destroyed it. My innocence turned to rubble that day. There were people who would want to kill other people they didn't know? And lots of them? And even small children? Everyone knew that on the second floor of the Alfred P. Murrah Federal Building there was a daycare. It was unfathomable.

In the middle of the chaos, I stood in the parking lot of the church, watching in disbelief. Bloody people being carried away. Children screaming. Cars burning. The church was so heavily damaged that we couldn't use it for months. But on that day, it was used as the on-site morgue. Every window in the entire building was blown out except the Jesus window, a large stained-glass window that became a symbol of hope for the entire city over the next year.

A week or two after the bombing, when businesses around the downtown area were trying to get back on their feet, we were allowed into our church to gather essentials. We then scrambled to try to find new offices and a place to worship. A Baptist church was kind enough to let us have morning services around its services. And we found some office space further into downtown, a few blocks from the rubble of the Murrah building.

However, life was not going on as usual. Men with assault rifles from what seemed like every law enforcement agency imaginable lined the streets and surrounded the scene of the crime. This included our church, which was thought to contain potentially important evidence from the explosion. Crime-scene tape fluttered in the wind for many blocks. Snipers paced on rooftops. I could see their silhouettes as I walked to and from my car for work. There were no smiles on their faces. They were stoic and steely-eyed. They watched my every move as if I could be another Timothy McVeigh. Any of us could, I guess, because he looked so. . .ordinary.

Since we didn't own any parking downtown other than our church parking lot, which now had the FBI mobile unit anchored in the middle of it, we had to park many blocks away from our offices. Every morning and every night, I trudged to and from work, staying on Broadway, a major street. All the while, I kept an eye on the men with guns so that I wouldn't accidentally cross the barrier tape. I saw them yell at people who tried to cross the tape to take shortcuts to their cars.

The bombing caused the vibrancy of downtown to quietly dwindle away for a while. People walked together but didn't talk. Wheels on cars hardly made noise. Nobody honked for you to move faster. All the regular sounds of a busy downtown faded into the dust and sorrow of the Murrah building.

One night I stayed late at work. I don't remember why, but I remember it was dark when I left. I walked briskly because the wind was a little cold. I passed the last corner where the crime-scene tape ended. I only had one more block to go before I reached the lot where we were allowed to park. A few cars passed on Broadway, but almost everyone was already home.

I remained vigilant, just as my parents always taught me. I knew a single female, no matter where she was, could be a target. But I wasn't scared. Until suddenly, about twenty yards up ahead of me, a man stood, blocking my path.

I didn't know how he got there. A brick building stood where he could have come out of a doorway, but there was no door. There was not any kind of alleyway or place where he could have hidden. Fear chilled my body. His eyes gleamed with menace even though he was smiling at me.

He wore a heavy, brown, leather duster, and he flashed it open, like he was showing me he had no weapons. He started to walk toward me. No one else was around. No car driving by. No people walking to their cars. Even the street lights around us seemed to dim, and I suddenly realized how black the night was.

I thought to myself, *RUN!* But I did nothing but stand still, frozen in my own shock, watching this man smile at me while feeling no warmth from him at all.

Then, like a flash, I saw another man. I thought, *Where did he come from?* There was still nothing but a brick wall ahead. He put his arms out, right on the other man's shoulders, and said quietly, "You don't want to do that," as he pushed the man to the wall.

All my primal survival instincts came back to me, and I ran. I darted out into the street, moving around the two men who were now just a blur as I passed them. Then I bolted back onto the sidewalk and ran all the way to the parking lot. But I had to turn. I had to see what was going on behind me. Just one glance, I told myself.

Out of breath, I stopped and looked back. There was nothing in that space but an empty sidewalk. The night had gone even quieter, like the air was holding its breath. My eyes darted to all the places they could've gone, but the only escape was across the street. And there was no one there.

I was too scared to investigate any further, so I went to my car. I sat there for a little bit, breathing hard, remembering that man's eyes. I never saw the face of the other man. His back was to me. But his voice was so calm. As I drove off into the night, I believed with every part of my being that I'd seen my very first angel. What the other man was, who could know?

Over the next few months, the city remained unsettled and not just in the disorder the bombing had caused through traffic and damage to numerous buildings many blocks away. The spirit of the city was heavy with sorrow and fear. As a youngster, I wasn't taught very much about the spiritual realm. But there was a palpable feeling of tension everywhere you went downtown, like a battle was being fought somewhere nearby even though you couldn't see it. I peered at each person who passed me, wondering if he or she was an angel in disguise.

One late afternoon, I left downtown, hitting five o'clock traffic right on the nose. I was on the entry ramp merging onto I-35, the busiest highway in the city, when I heard something thump against the bottom of my vehicle. And then the most horrible sound, like metal scraping against concrete, accompanied a sudden dragging on my car. I quickly pulled to the side of the highway, not knowing what I had hit.

In the days before cell phones, I sat for a moment, trying to figure out what to do. I had not had any kind of major car problems until that point in my life. I knew it could be dangerous for me to get in a car with a stranger. I wondered if a police officer might see me on the side of the road and stop to help.

What kept my attention most was how much my vehicle shook every time a car passed. When a semi roared past, it felt like I was about to be blown off the road. I watched my rear-view mirror for a chance to get out of my car, but the traffic just whizzed by, one car after the other. Nobody stopped, and I was given no chance to get out.

So, I climbed out the passenger side. I needed to see what was under my car. Maybe, just maybe, I could pull it out.

Against the wind of vehicles passing at seventy miles per hour, I dropped to my knees and peeked under the car. I could see what looked like a three-foot, metal pipe jammed into the undercarriage. I started to reach for it but then thought I heard a car pull over. I got off my knees to find a red pickup truck in front of my car and a man who was already out of his truck and walking toward me.

My breath caught in my lungs. If he was dangerous, should I just run for it? But as he got closer, I could see he was wearing an Oklahoma City Firefighters t-shirt and a hat to go with it. He said a friendly hello, and I was set at ease, not because of the friendly hello—any psycho can manage that—but because he was a firefighter. I explained the situation, and he dropped to his knees, rolled over, and scooted beneath my car. He was saying something about it, but I couldn't hear because of the highway traffic.

Finally, he emerged holding the pipe.

"I'm sure glad you didn't try to pull this out yourself," he said. "If you'd moved it forward to try to shake it loose, it would've punctured the. . ." He named the car part, but I didn't know what it was or care. All I knew was this man was a lifesaver! I dropped to my knees, wondering if anything was leaking out of the car. It looked fine. I hopped up and turned to thank him, but. . .he was gone. The truck was gone. I looked down the highway to see if I could spot his truck, but there was no red truck driving away. How could he have disappeared so quickly? I had glanced below my car for mere seconds.

I shook my head and looked up to God, thanking Him for sending what I was sure was another angel. I thought I was awfully fortunate to encounter angels twice in my lifetime and figured I'd never meet another one again, but God wasn't finished showing me all the ways an angel can help a human. The most extraordinary angel encounter was yet to come.

It was 2002, and I was a newly published author, trying to make a living off of novels but not quite making it. My husband, whom I'd met at the church that was destroyed by the bombing, took a job as a worship leader in south Oklahoma City. It became our home church, but I still liked staying connected to the downtown church for which I had so much affection. It was rebuilt from the bombing and was thriving again. For extra cash, I maintained the nursery there for the church's Bible studies twice a week.

During that time in my life, I was also full of zeal and excitement for the Lord. I was attending Bible studies as much as I could, and I was engaging with the Word constantly. I heard a sermon that really touched my heart. It was about how time is a commodity God can use if we let Him and about how we are not always willing to give Him our time when He wants it the most.

So, on a Tuesday morning, I remember praying hard, the kind of prayer where you're really focused and meaning every word you say to the Lord. I prayed, "God, today, my time is Your time. Whatever time You need from me, it's Yours." And then I got baby Cate dressed and helped my three-year-old son, John, get ready, too. We were out the door and on our way to work at First Church downtown.

Downtown was always an interesting place for me. I grew up in the country and graduated with less than one hundred people, so being around this large, thriving downtown was different for

me. I always felt a little more sophisticated there. A lot of home-
less people stopped by First Church, and we did what we could
to help them. Sometimes they wandered into the service looking
for help. Occasionally, they were so drunk that they had to be
removed. One man brought a chicken to service. He tried to hide
it under his coat.

I knew from experience that downtown could also be a dangerous place, so I was always on guard, especially if I was by myself.
I was more cautious than most because of my experience with the
man who had looked like he intended to do me harm.

Both kids were in car seats, which required me to duck into the
car and unlatch them. I always made sure I looked around to see
who was nearby before giving my attention to the inside of the car.
I knew those few seconds it took me to take the kids out made me
a vulnerable target, so it was always a little nerve-racking to get
the two kids out of the car.

On this particular day, John was already out, and I had Cate
on my hip. I gathered bags and reached for John's hand to make
sure he was near. I checked to be sure my keys were in my hand
before I locked the car and then headed toward the entrance.

"Excuse me?"

I turned around. An older woman, hunched and cloaked in
drab, mismatched clothes, peered at me as she grasped at a shawl.
Every piece of clothing she had on seemed to lack color. It was as
if she were a faded, sepia photograph in motion. She hardly moved
as she watched me turn around.

"Excuse me, ma'am?" she said.

I didn't say anything. But I was scared. I clutched Cate. Pulled
John close to me. Worked to keep my bags on my shoulder. I've
always been a sensitive person. I guess it is the artist in me. But I
never wanted to make anybody feel less than valuable. Sometimes
I disagreed with how we had to turn people away at our church,

but I understood we couldn't help them all. And many of them were indeed looking for money for alcohol rather than for food.

All these things ran through my mind like a bullet train as I tried to assess the situation. The woman didn't look dangerous at all. She wasn't even moving closer to me, though she was strangely close for me to have not heard her walk up.

What did she want? Money? I couldn't get to it without letting one of the kids out of my clutches. Whatever she needed, I couldn't risk it with the children. I would've handled it differently if I had been alone, but I had small kids with me.

She looked at me for a moment and then quietly asked, "Ma'am, do you have any time to spare?"

"No, no, I'm so sorry. I really am. I have the kids. I need to get to work. I'm very sorry. . ." I scooted John toward the building and turned, walking briskly as I tried to keep all my bags and nerves together. Only five seconds later, I stopped. My breath caught in my throat.

She said *time*. Time! I whirled around, eager to rush back to her. I did have time! I told God all my time was for Him! "I have time!"

But to my dismay, she was gone. I looked around. Surely, I could see the top of her head between the cars in the parking lot. She was right there just seconds ago. I sprinted forward with my bags hanging off my elbows, tugging John to follow.

"Ma'am? Ma'am?" I hollered.

But there was nobody—not a single soul—nearby. Like a vapor, she vanished.

I mourned that moment for many months and still feel sorrow about it to this day. What would've happened—I've asked myself over and over—if I had said yes?

It showed me just how meek a spiritual life I had. How earnestly I had prayed that morning. But given a chance less than an hour later, I'd already forgotten what I promised God!

Time passed, and one decade turned into two. My toddlers turned into teenagers. I rarely visit downtown anymore, but I will never forget that all three of my angel encounters happened there.

As far as I know, I've never encountered another angel. But I'm wise enough to believe the Scripture's warning that we should be hospitable to strangers because we might be entertaining angels unaware. And I certainly have moved past my childhood impressions of fluffy clouds and harp-playing beings with long, blond, flowing hair. I believe that, in their created state, angels are larger than we can comprehend because every time they arrive on earth, they have to tell humans not to be afraid. But, in their helping state, when they've intervened in one situation or another, they sure have a way of blending in while leaving a lifelong, indelible impression.

Rene Gutteridge is the award-winning author of twenty-four, multi-genre novels and a seasoned collaborator in fiction and film. She has novelized six screenplays and movies, including *Old Fashioned*, with writer and director Rik Swartzwelder. Her seven suspense books include *Possession*, *Misery Loves Company*, *Ghost Writer*, and *Escapement*.

Her indie film, the comedy *SKID* (available on Amazon Prime), was the deadCenter Film Festival's Best Oklahoma Feature Film Winner in 2015. Her novel *My Life as a Doormat* was adapted into a Hallmark film called *Love's Complicated*, which premiered in January 2016. She is the head writer for The Skit Guys.

CHAPTER THREE

SHE WROTE, "MIRACLE OF GOD" Dennis E. Hensley

The physician looked straight at me and said, "I'm really, really sorry, Dennis, but your baby is dead."

"Dead?" I echoed, utterly shocked. "How can the baby be dead when it hasn't even been born yet? This can't be true."

The doctor put a hand on my shoulder. "I cannot hear a heartbeat. I've had three nurses and another doctor listen, and they cannot hear a heartbeat other than your wife's. I've hooked two different fetal monitors onto the child inside the womb, and both have flatlined for five minutes each. I don't know why this happened. But I have to tell you, there is no doubt, the baby is dead."

I collapsed into a hard, plastic chair in the hospital hallway. I was thirty years old, and my wife, Rose, was twenty-nine. We had a three-year-old son who was as healthy as could be. And for the previous nine months, things seemed normal during each of my wife's check-ups. We had the new baby clothes all ready for the

29

new arrival. I went through the prenatal and birthing classes again so that I could be with my wife during the delivery. Everything was as it should be. . .until now. Right on the day of delivery, the physicians and nurses were telling me our baby was dead.

That was August of 1978. I had just finished my third year of doctoral studies at Ball State University in Muncie, Indiana, working toward a PhD in English. My wife and I had everything planned. I accepted a job as a public information officer at Manchester University in North Manchester, Indiana, and would start in three weeks. We were going to welcome the new baby, move to North Manchester, and get settled. Then I would begin working at my new job. It would provide me with a salary and benefits while also allowing me time to write my doctoral dissertation. But now all those plans faded as I stood there trying to comprehend what the physician just told me.

"What—what do we do. . .about this?" I rambled.

This obviously was not the first time the doctor had to answer that question. His responses were memorized, practiced, and so automatic they almost offended me, as though there was a ritual to follow.

"First, I think you need to be the one to go in and tell your wife about the situation. She's been in labor a long time, and she's exhausted and worried. She keeps asking why so many doctors and nurses keep coming in to examine her. We feel it would be best if you were the one to break the sad news to her. After that, maybe you can call some relatives or close friends to come and spend the next few hours with you. It may be another five hours before we actually extract the body."

Extract the *body*? Is that what he was calling it? That was my child he was talking about. He was making it sound like some sort of medical review process for interns to attempt.

"Then I'll need you to sign some forms so we can perform an autopsy to determine the exact cause of death. I know that sounds harsh, but it may help us learn something that could save another child's life sometime in the future. Other than that, it'll just be a matter of comforting your wife as much as possible until after the procedure."

Procedure? Extract the body? Was he afraid to say *birth* or *delivery*? Did this have to be so clinical? My heart was broken, and I still had to go in and tell my wife about—what did he called it?—"the situation."

I stalled by first calling our parents. We moved from Bay City, Michigan, to Muncie in 1975 because the program at Ball State would provide money to match my G.I. Bill benefits as a Vietnam veteran if I agreed to teach undergraduate students for three years while doing my doctoral work. Our relatives were still back in Michigan, but upon hearing the news of our tragedy, they said they'd leave as soon as possible to come be with us. It was a six-hour drive.

When I went in at last, I was crying, which was extremely rare for me. Rose's worst imaginings were instantly confirmed. "Something is wrong with the baby," she said. "What is it? No one will tell me anything. The baby hasn't been kicking for the past two hours. I've been worried something terrible has occurred."

I couldn't speak. We held hands, wept, and were silent. Finally, I cleared my throat and mumbled, "They—they don't know why, but the baby's heart stopped beating about an hour ago. They've double-checked it with monitors and got no readings. They've listened to you and can only hear your heartbeat. They want me—" I got choked up and had to take a moment to recover. "They want me to sign a permission form to allow them to perform an autopsy to find out what caused it."

The agony on Rose's face mirrored the pain I felt inside. We would have given our own lives to save our child, but that was not an option. After nine marvelously happy months awaiting the arrival of our new baby, we suddenly were alone, crying, and agonizing over a loss too great to bear.

In time, some friends from our church arrived, and one dear lady named Sandy Scott convinced me to go to the hospital chapel with her to pray. She said to me, "I know you, Dennis. You teach Sunday school, you serve as the missions' treasurer, and you even assist with children's church during evenings. I cannot help but think the Lord is putting you and Rose through this ordeal for a higher purpose. I don't know what that can be, but I want you to trust Him. This is all part of His plan."

I honestly could not see how the death of an innocent child could serve God's purposes in my life, especially when I was feeling as helpless and as hollow as it was possible to feel. I served for a year in Vietnam as a sergeant in the army, so I knew about losing close friends. But those men died serving a great cause. This baby. . .well. . .never even had a chance to accomplish anything.

Nevertheless, I prayed for spiritual strength. I also prayed for physical strength so that I could comfort my wife when I went in with her for the removal of the child. That came all too quickly. Before I knew it, I was dressed in green scrubs and seated next to my wife's head as they prepared her for the "extraction."

This was all so radically different from when my son was born in this same hospital three years earlier. On that day, I came into the delivery room with my wife, sat next to her by her head, coached her, and encouraged her while we both looked at mirrors that allowed us to see the birth of our little boy. It was unlike any experience we ever knew. Our joy was amplified as our relatives and close friends soon got to see our new child and rejoice in his birth with us.

Today, however, there was no rejoicing. This time, they turned away all the mirrors so that we would not have to witness the birth of our deceased child. The doctors and nurses were not laughing with us. The mood was somber, the room was silent, the movements were perfunctory.

The attending nurse, Mrs. White, opened the registry book in the room. Next to HENSLEY, I saw her print STILLBORN. My heart stopped beating for an eternity. Truly, again, I knew at that moment that if I could give my own life for my child, I gladly would. Also in that instant, it was as though a voice said to me, "Now you understand how it feels." And, yes, probably for the first time in my life, I truly understood the sacrifice the Father made in giving His only Son to die for my sins. It was a revelation that would stay with me forever.

The doctor and his two nurses began performing the delivery procedures. I sat next to my wife, stroking her hair and blotting her forehead. The medical team worked for about fifteen minutes, then suddenly I heard the doctor say, "That's impossible."

Then Mrs. White said, "That baby just wet on you. A baby cannot have bodily functions if it's dead. That baby is alive."

My wife was too exhausted to follow what was going on, but I heard every word as clear as a bell. I stood and took two steps toward the medical team, but the other assisting nurse, Miss Beckam, raised a hand and said, "Please, be seated, sir. And keep your mask on."

I could see the doctor whirl around and place our baby—a little girl, which was obvious to me—on a side table. I watched him insert a tube down the child's throat and squeeze on a hard, rubber balloon on the opposite end. The baby's lungs filled with air. The doctor released the balloon, and the child's lungs deflated.

"Here, take over," he ordered Mrs. White. "The baby can't breathe on her own. Keep a slow, steady rhythm." He turned to the other nurse. "Get on that phone. Call for Dr. Jasper. I need backup in here now!" He then turned back to caring for my wife. Within two minutes, another doctor and two more nurses arrived. They told me I'd have to leave.

"But what's going on?" I demanded. The doctor would not say. However, Mrs. White winked at me. She walked over to the registry book. As I watched, she crossed out the bold printed word "STILLBORN" and wrote above it MIRACLE OF GOD.

She pushed me toward the door. Before making me leave, she said, "The baby is alive but has a very, very faint heartbeat. She's too weak to breathe on her own, so we're doing that for her. We've called Riley Children's Hospital to send a special ambulance to take her to Indianapolis. I don't know if she'll make it, but I do know your dead daughter is now alive."

I walked into the hallway. I was in a daze. When friends asked what happened, I said, "She's alive."

Misunderstanding, they all said, "Rose was dying?"

"No, no," I said. "The baby. It's a little girl. She's alive. They say she's very ill, but she's alive."

There were tentative shouts of joy, tempered by the fact the child might yet die. I accepted a sandwich and a soft drink from someone, realizing I hadn't eaten in more than ten hours. My friends stayed by me, and after an hour we were told Rose had been taken into isolation because she lost a lot of blood in the delivery. After dressing me in a sterile, paper gown and covering my head and mouth, they let me go in to see her. But she was exhausted to the point of not being wholly conscious. I let her rest and sought a doctor.

"I have no explanation for it," the doctor said. "Five of us pronounced that baby dead, and two different fetal monitors confirmed no heartbeat. I don't believe in miracles, but I have no medical explanation for this."

The special ambulance arrived, and a pair of trauma nurses shared the task of pushing air into our child's lungs during the ninety-minute ride to the children's hospital. For the next twelve days, I drove down to see my daughter each afternoon, and every day she grew stronger. She was breathing on her own after two days. She began to suck a bottle after one week. Meanwhile, Rose, too, regained strength. And after ten days, she was released to go home. On day twelve, my wife, son, and I got to bring baby Jeanette home. The diagnosis was that she was born with a complete heart block. And even though she survived, her heart would always beat every other time.

After the celebratory hoopla calmed down, the endless stream of visitors finished coming to our home to see the "miracle baby," and our relatives all went back to Michigan, I had time to be alone. It was then that my prayers bordered on bitterness. Yes, I was overwhelmingly grateful my daughter was alive. But I could not help but feel puzzled and even angry that God had played such a "sick joke" on my wife and me. "Your baby is dead. Whoops, uh, not really." What kind of a warped God would inflict such needless agony on a couple who had served Him well?

During those times of soul-searching, Sandy Scott's words continually came back to me, echoing her message that God had a purpose in all this. I also could remember hearing those words, "Now you understand how it feels."

A full year passed, and our family doctor, a woman in her early thirties, became pregnant with her first child. We were truly happy for her. Each time we brought our children in for check-ups, we'd ask her how she was doing, and she was always eager to say she was in great health and excited about the arrival of her child.

We were stunned when word reached us the day of her delivery. Her little son only lived for nine hours. The umbilical cord was wrapped around his neck in the womb, leading to complications that took his life. Our grief for our doctor was immense. But things got worse when we called to make our next appointment: we were told our doctor gave up her practice, went into a deep emotional depression, and wouldn't even come out of her house. She considered herself a failure as a mother and as a physician. No one could convince her otherwise.

Suddenly, I realized the importance of the words "Now you understand how it feels." I took a pen and some paper and wrote a long, personal letter to our doctor. I explained exactly how she was feeling—hollow, impotent, lonely, and useless. I talked about anger and bitterness and frustration. I also talked about love and purpose and service. I quoted lines from Isaiah for her, explaining the eyes of the Lord look to and fro, seeking those who are called to His special purpose.

I concluded the letter by writing, "I now know why I had to be hurt so severely a year ago. It was so I'd be able to talk to you. There is a purpose for pain. You are an excellent doctor and during your lifetime career you will deliver a lot of babies. Not all of them will live. And when the parents turn to you and say, 'You don't understand,' you'll be able to say, 'Oh, I do, I truly do,' and you'll be able to minister to them in a way no other doctor could ever know how. I'm sorry we both had to be hurt so deeply, but I'm also honored the Lord would call us to such a level of service for him. You must go back to your practice. We all need you."

Two days later, this woman called me on the phone. She said, "You were the only one I would listen to. No one else understood. And because of your letter, yes, I'm going back to my career as a physician."

I am now sixty-eight years old. Two years ago, I saw in the paper that doctor retired after many decades as a family physician. Oh, and my daughter Jeanette? She is now a school teacher in Elkhart, Indiana, with a husband and two healthy kids of her own.

She had a pacemaker put in when she was thirty-two, and she's doing just fine.

Dr. Dennis E. Hensley is a professor at Taylor University and the author of more than sixty books, including *Jesus in the 9 to 5* (AMG Publishers) and *Jesus in All Four Seasons* (Bold Vision Books).

CHAPTER FOUR

SHE BELONGS TO HIM
JENNIFER L. PORTER

"Why would you sit in the backseat?"

The passenger seat remained empty. I lifted my novel in the air as explanation. Mom usually loved seeing me read, but this time she knew I was using the newest John Jakes novel to shut her out.

"Suit yourself." She gave me a quick look over her shoulder. "I don't care where you sit."

Surrounded by camping equipment and supplies, I pulled my bare feet onto the seat and promptly lost myself in another historical fiction adventure.

My eyes lifted when my mother reached back and touched my knee with a gentle pat. "Get your sandals on, dear. You clean the windshield while I pump the gas."

With a sigh, I folded down the corner of the page and looked up at the windshield. "Eew." Three plum-sized splats on the glass ended a week-long silent treatment. "Bug guts—looks like gooey boogers. Gross."

Mom looked surprised that I had spoken to her, but she replied in a matter-of-fact tone: "Nope, just grasshopper guts." She laughed at her own response, a deep chuckle ending in a mischievous giggle. The sound made me smile, but I didn't let her see it.

Sighing again, I unfolded my aching legs and slid on my sandals. "Knees hurting again?"

I nodded, stretching my aching legs with a groan before placing my feet on the hot cement.

Mom rubbed her own knees sympathetically. "Growing eight inches in two years will do that. They'll hurt for a while."

I looked into her pale blue eyes and envied her dark, even tan. I never tanned.

Frowning, I dunked the sponge and squeegee into the wash bucket before tuning out Mom's comments about how she grew six inches over one summer. I had heard the story over and over, and it brought little comfort when I experienced the exact same agony in my fourteenth summer. Since then, I had grown another two inches for a total of eight. As if I weren't skinny enough after the first growth spurt.

I looked at the remains of the grasshoppers and started scrubbing.

"Thanks, dear," Mom said, wiping her forehead with a towel. "It must be ten degrees hotter than predicted."

Heat waves shimmered off the hood of our green Dodge Aspen with fake wood panels on the sides. I knew to be careful not to let my exposed midriff touch the hot metal.

When I finished, I opened the back door and heard, "Ride in the front seat, please."

I knew it wasn't a request. Rubbing my knees, I slid onto the hot, sticky vinyl. Dropping a beach towel in my lap, Mom said, "Lay this on the seat."

Once we were back on the road, she put her hand in the middle of my book and pressed it into my lap. "Why the silent treatment?"

I shrugged, and she pointed at me. "Listen, I am not spending two weeks with you in this funk."

"You know why I'm angry." I looked at her. "Why do you hate my friends?"

She flipped the left turn signal and gave me a look. "Frankly, Jennifer Lynne, I don't like who you become when you are with them."

"I knew it." The words I'd been practicing in front of the mirror flew out of my mouth. "My own mother doesn't like me, that's rich."

Taking her eyes off the road for a moment, she glared, her knuckles going white on the steering wheel.

"Enough." The word exploded from her lips, and instantly I regretted repeating the words my friend used effectively against her own mother. I should have known better.

Instantly contrite, I lifted both hands. "I'm sorry."

Letting a slow breath escape through her parted lips, she patted my knee again. "That is the sort of behavior I'm talking about."

I repeated a quick sorry and she shook her head. "Do you want to know why I don't like your friends?"

I wasn't sure I wanted to know, so I tried diversion: "What's for dinner?"

"Nice try, brat." She laughed, giving me a light swat with the back of her hand. She always used brat affectionately, and I watched as she ran the same hand through her newly permed hair.

"You asked," she said, using her teacher voice, "so I'm gonna tell you."

I braced myself as she continued.

"You came home about a year ago with a five-inch chunk of hair cut from the back of your head. Your best friend asked if she could trim your dead ends. Remember?"

"I remember," I said slowly.

"What did she say? 'Oops!'" Mom let out a bitter laugh. "Oops, the scissors slipped. What a liar."

Weakly, I defended the girl. "She said she was sorry."

"Ohh," Mom said, nodding. "She was sorry, all right! Sorry you were getting prettier every day."

Well—at least Mom thought I was pretty.

She wasn't finished. "I've known girls like that my entire life. They choose friends who make them look better. When she met you, you'd just gone through a six-inch growth spurt, so you were skinny and a little awkward."

"I'm still skinny and awkward. And ugly."

"Stop it. You have never, ever been ugly."

I ran my tongue over my mangled front tooth and quietly disagreed.

"Your stuck-up friend butchered your hair. Why are you still friends with her?"

I looked out the window. "She. . .said she was sorry, so I forgave her."

I could hear Mom's frustration in her quickened breathing. "Well, you can be thankful for one thing," she said.

"What?"

"She could have stabbed you in the back while she was hacking off your hair."

"Funny, Mom."

Staring out the passenger window, I watched a black squirrel chase another up the heavily shaded trees. Sighing, I pulled my bare feet onto the seat before wrapping both arms around my pale white legs.

I dropped my head to my knees when Mom continued.

"And which one of their mothers called you garbage?"

The memory washed over me, and I tasted hot bile in my throat. "Never mind. She actually called me white trash. And worse."

My mother punctuated each of her next words. "That witch said, 'Get that white trash out of my house.' What kind of ignoramus calls any child, any person, *trash*?"

"Ignoramus?" I asked, not knowing the word.

"Dimwit, numbskull, know-nothing."

I nodded, adding the insult to my vocabulary arsenal.

"Seriously, who does she think she is, anyway?" Mom's words sprayed like a fire hydrant. "Don't mess with my kids. Hurt me, and I'll forgive you. Hurt my kids, and I will despise you until the day I die!"

I'd heard that threat my entire life, and this time was no different. Still, was she angry on my behalf? It made me sorry I'd been punishing her the whole week.

"Think about how I felt," she said, letting out a long sigh.

As we entered the small town of Andover, Ohio, she lowered her speed. "I just can't believe she called my sweet girl trash, not because of anything you'd done, but because of our house and the street we live on. Un-be-lieve-able!" The word escaped through gritted teeth.

"Mom," I moaned, "please stop." She'd made her point.

"What was the reason she gave for kicking you out of her house?"

I sighed, knowing Mom wouldn't stop until she was good and ready to. "She said, 'I know everything I need to know about you because I know where you live.'"

Mom jerked her chin downward in an emphatic nod. "I know you wanted to bring your friend to camp, but this is my vacation, too."

"I get it," I said, no longer defensive. "But I don't have friends at school. Those friends you don't like are the only ones I've got."

"If you can count five true friends on one hand at the end of your life, you are truly blessed. I promise, those kids will not make the cut."

"But everyone teases me because I'm skinny and have frizzy hair." Mom remained quiet, so I went on. "Did you know I pick spitballs out of my hair every single day at school?"

Mom never entertained self-pity, so she changed the subject. "Corn on the cob, hamburgers, and potato chips."

When I gaped in confusion, she smiled. "You asked what we were having for dinner. We good?"

I nodded. "Yeah, we're good."

Over the years, I made friends with several girls within a two-block radius of our campsite. When I saw Valerie's family pull up in their pickup truck, I ran into the camper.

"Vallie's here. Can I go?"

Mom, who was working on her master's degree, looked up. "You know the rules."

"Yep, buddy system."

"Let me know what you decide to do."

After a quick wave, I ran across the thick gravel to the campsite two streets over. The newcomers were tidying up the area when I reached them. "Hey, can I help?"

Her father gave me a quick hug and handed me a rake. "Vallie, Jennifer's here."

Valerie appeared, her hands covered with gardening gloves and her face set in annoyance. "Dad, call me Val."

I grinned. "My friends call me Jennie with an 'ie.'"

Her dad laughed. "Val and Jennie with an 'ie,' I'm going to sit for a while."

I gave Val a hug, and we tackled every job at top speed so that we could go to the pool and the new teen center. My friend had blossomed into a beautiful girl and didn't care that I still looked like a feminine version of a pre-pubescent boy. In record time, leaves were bagged, flowers were planted, and firewood was stacked. Her dad finally gave us the okay to leave. Valerie pulled off the gardening gloves and looked at me. "Get your bathing suit and towel, then meet me back here, 'kay?"

"Okay."

After an afternoon of swimming, I was glad to change into dry clothes and investigate the teen center. Giant speakers blasted KC and The Sunshine Band's "That's the Way (I Like It)," and Val taught me how to dance "the bump." The large rectangular room held rows of new pool tables, video games, and a full dance floor. I wasn't a good dancer, but now I could do the bump.

We were walking back at sunset when we passed a roaring bonfire. The smell of wood smoke hung heavily in the air, and a cute guy called out, "Hey, come join us."

A large group of teenagers sat around the fire, and they waved us in. They seemed so friendly.

"Yeah, join us!"

"Plenty of room."

Val and I looked at each other and laughed, marveling that these older kids were asking us to join them.

"Sure." Val walked over and found a seat beside the cutest boy.

I figured I was invited because of my beautiful friend, but they were nice to me, too, and even laughed at my jokes.

"This bonfire is humongous," I said, stating the obvious while using one of my newest vocabulary words. "This must be five or six times larger than any fire we've ever made. Impressive."

My brothers would have made fun of my stupidity, but this group agreed with me and went into detail about how they constructed the bonfire.

The flames burned so hot that the leaves above us curled and darkened as the blaze and sparks rose. We kept changing position as the smoke wafted in our direction. Raising their voices over the roar of the fire, the other kids took turns telling spooky stories. And I found myself mesmerized by the red sparks that danced like feathers on the heat waves.

Flicking on the flashlight tied to my bag, I checked my watch and remembered my curfew. The time had flown by.

"I've got to get back before midnight." It'd been a long day and Valerie agreed it was time to leave.

"Same time tomorrow?" A handsome guy smiled at us. He appeared to be about the same age as my older brothers—maybe nineteen or even twenty.

"You're having another bonfire tomorrow? Here?"

I was thrilled.

"What do you think?" I looked at Val. "Do you want to come back?"

Val laughed. "Duh." She'd been flirting with one of the younger guys and gave him a coy wave.

We agreed to meet them the next night and giggled the whole way back to camp. "This is going to be the best summer ever."

~

Mom was in our pavilion with lights strung around the inside. I unzipped the flap and rushed in to tell her about the giant, no, humongous bonfire.

"We were invited tomorrow night, too. Can I go?"

Val chimed in. "Please?"

Mom sat back and looked at us. "Back before midnight?" she asked.

"Of course." I said, laughing. Midnight was the cut-off; anything later would be met with certain grounding.

"Yay!" we squealed.

"Thanks, Mom, you're the best." I leaned over and gave her a kiss and was rewarded with a hug. Excited to have found some new friends at camp, I told her everything I could remember about our night.

"Mom, they were so nice. They even shared their potato chips and pop." For some reason this generosity struck me.

"That's nice, honey."

Val drawled, "The bonfire was huge, man." She drew out "maaahhn," sounding like the kids at the fire, who used "man" as punctuation for nearly every sentence. Mom lifted a brow and looked over her glasses. I could tell she was sizing up my old friend with thirteen years of teacher's intuition. My brothers called Mom's stare "the hairy eyeball." It was enough to make Val ditch the cool act and stutter, "A, yes, a big fire, Mrs. Mink."

After seeing a sign of respect, she smiled and Val relaxed.

"Buddy system?" We answered her question with eager nods. This was a must at camp, especially when we went swimming or were on the lake. The mandatory buddy rule was also the reason I helped Val clean her yard. I wasn't allowed to go anywhere by myself.

"Vallie is going with me."

"Obviously," Mom drawled, looking at the two of us. "Stay together and don't make me come looking for you." This was a real warning.

As Val flipped on the flashlight to walk back to her camp lot, we yelled back and forth, "Best summer ever."

—

The next day, Val did my hair and make-up in the tiny camper bathroom. I felt pretty because she found a way to partially tame my fuzzy mane. As we walked to the party, a guy from the bonfire drove up. Popping his head out the window opening, he said, "Hey, man. Why walk when you can ride, man?"

Val pushed me toward the car. I looked toward camp and back at my friend, shaking my head no.

"Jenn, get in," Val insisted. "I'm not walking."

I didn't want to get into trouble. "That's okay. I can walk. I'll see you there."

Val got into the car. "Come on, Jenn."

"I'm really not allowed. . ." I didn't know why I was so nervous. I did a little drinking and smoking with my friends from home, so what could be wrong with accepting a ride with this guy?

Trust your intuition. My mother's warning rang in my head. *Be ever mindful of your surroundings.*

I looked back at the campsite, but Mom wasn't there to stop me.

"Come on." Val got out of the car and pushed me toward the open door. "Get in. You don't have to tell your mother everything."

I sighed and slid into the car. A minute later I was alarmed when the driver didn't turn right at the main road.

"Whoa, wait," I said. "I thought we were going back to the bonfire near the teen center."

Clearly, we were heading toward the camp entrance. Why did I get in this car?

"I can't leave the campgrounds," I protested. "Let me out."

I felt a hand push me back against the seat. With a sly grin on her face, Val said, "Relax, Jennie. It will be fun." It was as if she knew the party was somewhere else. Maybe she did. Why did I think I knew her? We hadn't seen each other in a whole year. My heart threatened to beat out of my chest.

"Let me out of this car!" I yelled. "I can't leave the campground! You don't understand. My mother will kill me."

I tried to talk to each of the guys in the car, but they wouldn't even look at me.

"I'll walk back. Really, let me out here." They ignored me and the driver kept driving. Leaning forward, I cried, "Please, stop. I really need to get out. I'm serious. I'll walk from here."

The guy didn't respond. Val was sitting by the door, and when I reached for the handle, she blocked me. I smacked her hand away.

"Sit back and shut up, Jennifer." She shot me a killing look. I closed my mouth and sat back as alarm filled my heart. I'd read enough mystery books to know I needed to pay attention to where we were going. The scenery flew by, dark green trees on the left and swampland on the right; we were heading south toward the town of Andover.

When we reached the causeway, the car turned left onto the bridge where my brothers and cousins fished. A large Welcome to Pennsylvania sign passed by. Not only had I left Holiday Camplands, they were taking me across the state line.

"Why won't you let me out of the car?" My heart was pumping hard. My plea was met with silence and a glare from my friend. Panic set in as I focused on the choppy water below the causeway. I stole a look at Valerie. She seemed amused at my discomfort and not nervous at all.

Was this what teenagers did? I didn't know; I'd never been invited to a cool kids' party. I'd heard the true test of a great party was if you puked your guts out, but I didn't know anything else.

We turned onto a back road, and after a few minutes we pulled onto a long, gravel driveway. The short grass was burned from the hot, dry summer. A tiny saltbox house stood back from the road, much smaller than my house. Closing my eyes, I tried to remember directions and road signs. If I left as soon as we stopped, I might make it back to the visitor center before dark.

Smoke blew toward the gravel driveway. "At least the part about the bonfire was true," I said. No one answered as I got out of the car and looked around. How was I going to get out of here?

Val walked ahead of me with the confidence of a natural beauty. I swore bitterly as I watched her, and then I scanned the dark woods surrounding the house. Behind me was a guy from the car, and I swore again as he shoved me into the living room. Pungent smoke hung like smog in the room, and I started to cough, my eyes watering. Squinting while I wiped away tears with the back of my hand, I studied the kids lining the walls. Most of them weren't much older than me. Was anyone else brought here against his or her will?

As I examined the rectangular room, my horror mounted when I spotted bowls of blue and red pills sorted like M&M'S. A large basket of tightly woven joints was set at the end of the table, and I had no trouble identifying the odor filling the stuffy space. I could hear my mother's voice inside my head: *Don't eat or drink anything offered to you.*

"Take all you want," a guy said, waving his hand over the drugs like a magician. "Everything's free." I watched as Val jammed a handful of pills into the pocket of her shorts before dropping into an empty spot on the floor.

"Are you crazy?" I sat next to her and hissed in her ear. "What if the police come?"

"Shut up, man. You're embarrassing me."

I gritted my teeth and swore at her.

"Just shut up, Jenn." Pushing her long chestnut hair behind her ear, Val turned away and waved at the boy from the night before. Obviously, she regretted befriending me again. Well, the feeling was mutual.

"Oh yeah, best summer ever," I said loud enough for her to hear. She flipped me off, and I returned the gesture.

Her new boyfriend came over and reached out to help her off the floor. She got up with a big smile, swinging her hips as she walked away. I shook my head as he led her through a door directly across from where I was sitting.

At first I couldn't figure out what I was seeing. A room full of pigs, perhaps? I blinked and blinked again. I'm sure my mouth fell open—the room was filled with naked bodies.

What was I seeing?

I couldn't pull my gaze from what looked like a perverted game of Twister with bodies interwoven and writhing. Someone kicked the door shut, and I was glad to close my eyes. I'd heard about orgies and was surprised Val didn't even hesitate to enter that room. Maybe she had dropped acid or popped a few of those pills. . .

I whispered the prayer I had heard many times in movies: "God, if You get me out of here, I'll serve You forever." I was not going into that room.

You think you know somebody. My mother's advice about poor choices made me wince, and I argued with her in my head.

But, Mom, I've known Vallie for years. How could I know?

An involuntary shudder shook my entire frame. I shook my head to rid the image from my brain.

I had to find a phone.

Getting up from the floor, I moved past the table of drugs and into a tiny kitchenette. No one looked up, probably because they were already stoned.

No phone. How could a place in the country not have a phone? Everybody had a phone, didn't they? No phone book either. The cabinets were empty. Who would I call anyway? The guardhouse at Holiday Camplands? Maybe the police? What would these people do if they heard me calling the police?

"Oh God." The words weren't a prayer; they were an oath of despair. Mom thinks I'm near the teen center. She won't know I'm gone, or dead, until long after midnight.

How could there be no phone?

From the back step of the small house, I took stock of my surroundings. No neighbors on either side. Figures. It was a dark, moonless night, and I counted four men standing watch in the backyard. No wonder they had lookouts.

Inhaling the night air with a shaky breath, I walked toward the bonfire. Gathered in a circle to my right were kids chanting in low tones. I couldn't understand what they were saying, nor did I care. No one noticed me, and I gave them a wide berth. I jumped at the sound of several, loud bangs. Someone rolled firecrackers in newspaper and placed them on the edge of the fire. The pops sounded one after another, keeping me on edge.

I heard a laugh and saw a guy smoking near the trees. I figured he was another lookout. I moved to the other side of the fire so that he couldn't see me. I was used to being invisible, and for the first time I was thankful to be plain and painfully thin.

What if the police came? How could I prove I wasn't part of all this? Transporting a minor across the state line, that was kidnapping, right? I began to hope the police would come. I felt better outside and kept an eye on the driveway and the chanters by the fire. Surely someone would be leaving? With so many kids crammed into the tiny house, you'd expect to see cars or dirt bikes. Everyone seemed to have dirt bikes at camp. How did all these people get here? Where were their vehicles?

I have no idea how long I sat by the fire, but finally a car pulled into the driveway. Instantly on my feet, I ran across the uneven ground and pounded hard on the car's window.

"Hey, will you please take me back to Holiday Camplands? If I'm not back by midnight, my mother is going to knock me through a wall and paint over me," I asked the guy behind the wheel. "Please, I've got to get back."

The driver cracked the window. "I'm not leaving. You're out of luck."

"Please," I begged, determined to find a way home. I wasn't sure I could find my way back in the dark, but I wasn't staying there any longer.

Someone behind me spoke: "You're not going anywhere."

The voice was deep and threatening. I turned and saw a row of teenagers lit by the car's headlights. Valerie was with them. She was disheveled and glassy-eyed, but at least she had clothes on. I shook my head to rid the memory of her in the pig room. This couldn't be real.

"You're not going anywhere," he repeated.

"No, no, no, no, no." I didn't know what I was saying; I only knew I wasn't staying in that place. "You don't understand. I have to get back. My curfew is midnight." The thought of disappointing my mother was nearly as distressing as finding myself stranded in this hellhole.

The man moved toward me. Dark hair hung lank and greasy alongside a thin, twisted face. Wait, I remembered this guy. He was the hunk we thought was so cute. What was his name? Jimmy? No, he said his name was Jamie.

How could I ever have thought this guy was handsome? He was disgusting. As I watched, a worm-like bulge moved across his forehead. Maybe they'd slipped me drugs after all.

I stepped back, repulsed. What the heck was that? What would cause such a thing? It was as if a monster lived beneath his skin.

What had I gotten myself into?

To my surprise, the anger on Jamie's face suddenly disappeared. He backed up as if terrified of me. It didn't make sense. I stared at his horrified face as he and his friends recoiled like they'd seen a ghost. Jamie's face morphed again, and I thought the effect might be due to the lights of the car. But the stark fear on his face was unmistakable.

I looked behind me and saw nothing but the idling car. The driver was leaning on the open door, but he also reacted in terror when I faced him. What would cause these people to fear me? I weighed ninety pounds soaking wet.

And what was happening to Jamie's face?

Resignation underlined his next statement. "Let her go," he said with no trace of malice or anger. "She belongs to Him." Jamie spat out the word "Him" with bitterness. And with a casual wave of his hand, he let me go.

I didn't know who *Him* was, but I didn't stop to question anyone. I looked at my old childhood friend. "Vallie, come with me. These are bad people. This is a bad place."

She stepped forward, her face filled with disgust. "I knew you were a goody two shoes. I'm staying with my real friends."

"All right," I said. I felt guilty for leaving her. But self-preservation took over, and I slid into the car's back seat.

"Take her back," Jamie ordered the driver. I couldn't believe it. Without speaking, the driver took me back to our family's camper. I was relieved but couldn't shake the fear that settled into my soul. I'd seen and felt the heavy darkness of evil all around me.

Mom wasn't back at the camper yet, and I was not staying there by myself.

What if they came back for me?

~~~

Laughter and music filled the air as I crossed the street to join the Londons, our neighbors, around their fire. I leaned down to give my mom a kiss. Whew. The Londons were singing old spirituals in harmony, and Mary, Pastor Chris London's wife, made room for me before wrapping her arms around my shoulders.

"Goodness, girl, you have grown again."

"I'm five foot seven now," I replied, my teeth chattering. I was cold to the core and couldn't stop shaking. Mary draped a warm blanket over my shoulders, and I began to relax.

"Thank you, Mary."

"Come by tomorrow. Help me cut vegetables, and I'll put some meat on those bones." My stomach rumbled as I thought about the wonderful meals Mary cooked. She was beautiful and seemed to glow from the inside. Her skin, the color of extra-creamy, milk chocolate, was sprinkled from head to toe with freckles.

"Want me to braid this?" She ran her hand through my hair, and I nodded, knowing she'd create a tight French braid that would make my hair wavy in the morning.

Pulling rubber bands from a pocket in her dress, she grabbed a section of my hair. "White folks don't know what to do with hair like yours."

Mary grinned at my mother, who laughed and agreed.

As the music played, she crooned in my ear, asking the Lord to take her hand through the storm and through the night. . .

As Mary finished the braid, she kissed the top of my head. I felt tears roll down my cheeks. She was one of the dear souls who talked to me about Jesus, and for the first time that evening, I felt safe and warm.

~

The next morning, I went to Valerie's and found her family campsite closed for the winter. I looked at the flowers we had planted the day before and then peered through the trailer windows. The family was gone.

What the heck—why did they leave?

Her family came for two weeks but left after only one day? I knew I should have made her come back with me.

That afternoon, fear kept me in the camper reading or visiting with Mary across the street.

Valerie lived near my grandma, Helen. So when I visited a few months later, Val's dad picked me up, and the three of us went to Denny's.

As Valerie's father sat in a nearby booth, Valerie told me Jamie, a satanic priest, didn't remember saying, "Let her go. She belongs to Him."

But after I left, the group panicked, and their wrath fell on her. To them, it was as if I had vanished into thin air. They called her "damaged goods" and told her they wanted the blonde, green-eyed virgin instead.

"They took turns raping me." Val spoke without emotion, and I couldn't respond. Her father sat in the other booth with his back to us, unable to face us even though he heard every word.

Valerie went on, saying they used her in a ritual where they all sucked on her, leaving blood blisters all over her body. Then, when the coven was finished, she was dumped naked on her camper deck before sunrise. When her parents found her, embarrassed by their wild daughter, they shut down their campsite and went home.

When she finished describing her nightmare, she looked directly at me. "You're in danger. They promised to find you."

I was frightened after that summer night, but Valerie's story left me petrified. All the scary movies I had watched, séances I had attended, and books I had read indicated that I really could be in danger. I didn't think I'd ever be able to feel safe again.

I left Valerie and her father with much to think about. My parents taught me that good and evil were human characteristics rather than spiritual forces. After my experience, I came to the conclusion that evil was way more powerful than good.

But then, oddly enough, the woman I babysat for became a Jesus freak!

She was always saying, "Jesus loves you, Jesus died for your sins, and Jesus is the way, the truth, and the life." I was sick of hearing it.

With her, everything was about Jesus. But she noticed I was always afraid. After babysitting, I would run as fast as I could from her house to mine. I didn't like to go out after dark. When she remarked on my fearfulness, I finally told her about what had happened at the Lake Pymatuning camp.

Even after hearing my story, she wasn't afraid at all.

Grabbing a notebook from the table, she flipped to a clean page and drew a circle that filled the page. "Imagine this is God."

"Okay." I rolled my eyes at her simplistic approach. "So, God is a giant circle?"

"For some reason," she continued as if talking to a small child, "you think the devil is equal to God. You believe the devil rules hell while God rules heaven, right?" She stared at me until I answered.

"Seriously, I don't know if I believe anything," I said, having forgotten my panicked pledge to serve God forever.

"You are terrified, so it's clear you believe in something."

"This is crazy. Who discusses stuff like this?"

"Look at this circle again." She drew two more circles within it. "Imagine this is the Father, Son, and Holy Spirit." Then she drew a tiny little angel next to the big circle.

"Jennifer, the devil can never, ever be equal to God the Creator. Satan is equal in power to Gabriel or Michael, but he does not have the power of God on his side."

I liked what I was hearing, but I didn't believe it.

"The devil has already lost."

I stared in disbelief. This was the first time I was hearing this. The cartoon devil was always stronger than the wimpy, pathetic god masquerading as our conscience. In movies, the priest was easily tossed across the room before being impaled by a cross. Nope, the devil was much scarier and more powerful.

"I believe Jesus saved you on that night."

I nodded. Her words made sense, but why? "Why would God save me? That's illogical."

"Come to Bible study with me," she pleaded. "One time." She paused then promised, "After that, unless you want me to, I will never mention Jesus to you again."

"Deal," I said.

About a week later, we arrived at the Bible study. I pulled Nancy's baby girl out of the old car and kicked the rusting car door, neglecting to remove my hand from the opening. Dumb, I know. My fingernail instantly turned black, and the pain was so excruciating I was glad I hadn't dropped the baby. Tears ran down my face as I looked at my poor swollen finger. I told her I wanted to go home, but it was February and too cold to walk.

Kissing her daughter's head, Nancy said, "No. You promised."
I was angry and tried to call my mother several times. No luck.
Nancy was not taking me home. What a jerk.

Weak at the knees and feeling sick as the pain radiated through
my hand, I sat in the living room and waited for the Bible study to
end. Had I known this was a grandma Bible study, I never would
have agreed to come. Nearly every person in the room was ancient.

"I'm Beverly." The woman had short, red hair and a kind face.
"Sorry about your finger," she winced and examined my hand.
"Looks bad. Probably going to need a splint." Her eyes were filled
with compassion, and I felt tears welling up again. Handing me a
bag of ice, she tilted her head. "For the swelling."

"Thanks."

The woman next to me shook her head after looking at my
hand. She looked younger than the others; I guessed she was about
thirty.

Beverly said, "Shh, open your Bibles, please. Let's begin with
prayer." As Beverly's prayer came to an end, she said, "I'm sure you
noticed our new friend, Jennie, slammed her finger in the car
door." I looked up, surprised she was talking about me.

"Please, let's pray for her healing."

I groaned quietly and stared at the black nail, unable to believe
these archaic dingbats were praying for my finger. Who prays for
a finger?

But in that exact moment, my finger stopped hurting, and the
bruising and swelling disappeared. This was the same finger that
had been caught in the door of a dilapidated sedan.

Dumbfounded, I stared at the finger as though it didn't belong
to me. I felt no pain, none at all. The nail was still black, but the
swelling was gone.

Had I really hurt it as bad as I thought?

I pushed on the black nail bed to test it.

No pain. Nothing. I applied more pressure to the nail as the younger woman next to me said, "I'm Linda. God healed your finger, didn't He? It doesn't hurt anymore, does it?" She smiled at me, her eyes sparkling with joy and awe.

How did she know?

But I wasn't ready to accept the miracle. I lied and said, "Of course it hurts; I slammed it in a car door." To think God loved me enough to heal my finger was insane, wasn't it?

I had to be losing touch with reality.

Could God heal me?

Had He?

I began to earnestly listen to the woman leading the Bible study. The group was discussing eternity. I was intrigued by the idea but skeptical. I don't remember anyone ever talking about eternity, except maybe Bugs Bunny on his frequent trips to heavenly clouds. I thought the conversation was whacked, but I was willing to listen because God had healed my finger.

That night, I invited Jesus into my heart again. I prayed the same prayer I had prayed when I was young, but I never knew what to do afterward. I didn't feel any different.

But when I opened my eyes the morning after the Bible study, I knew I was changed. Indescribable joy eliminated the crippling fear that had been my constant companion during the past seven months. With each breath, I became aware of the loving presence filling my entire being.

I'm not afraid!

Linda told me that I'd become a new creation. That morning, I believed her and was overwhelmed with thankfulness for the peace I felt.

One might say that having my finger healed was the miracle. But to me, it was a catalyst meant to open my eyes and ears so that I would see and hear the truth. Like Dorothy in *The Wizard of Oz*, my world transformed from darkness to light, grayscale to living color. I knew life would never be the same.

After that night, Linda Fiorelli, a thirty-year-old hairstylist, became my spiritual mother. She talked to me at length about what had happened at Lake Pymatuning. It was clear God had protected me, but why? Why me, and for what purpose? Why did that face-morphing Jamie let me go? What did he see that terrified him and his friends?

Linda suggested that I keep my conversion a secret until I grew in the faith, explaining I was like a tender plant others would try to rip out. Her advice made sense, and I agreed. She began pouring her life into mine, teaching and training me to trust in the Lord.

By the time my friends realized the Jennie they knew was "born-again," I'd become a dyed-in-the-wool, flower in my hair, Bible-carrying Jesus freak. To my former friends, I became a Scripture-quoting alien who made certain each of them knew about the loving nature of our Supreme Creator and the sacrifice of Jesus, His only Son.

Yep, they hated me. But their disdain was a small price to pay for the peace ruling my heart.

As the school year drew to a close, I got a phone call from Fred, an old friend, asking me to be a designated driver. A lot of kids were going to a party.

"Please, Jennie, will you drive?" he asked. After all, I was a Jesus freak and wouldn't be getting stoned.

"Nope, sorry," I said quickly. "I have plans tonight."

I felt proud of myself as I hung up the phone. I couldn't think of a greater waste of my time. Tapping a book with the tips of my fingers, I did have plans to read.

"As if Jesus would want me to go to a kegger." I laughed. "Unthinkable. Ridiculous. Lord, can you believe them? Partying and drinking were two of the reasons I quit hanging out with that group in the first place."

I guess I expected a "way to go, good and faithful servant."

Not what I heard at all. Not in an actual voice, but in a strong feeling. A clear sense that Jesus wasn't happy with my decision to stay home, no matter how good the book was.

"You want me to drive?" I began to argue with the Lord. I knew whose voice I was hearing. After all, Jesus said, "My sheep listen to my voice; I know them, and they follow me" (John 10:27, NLT).

It wasn't until after I had become a churchgoer that I learned my prayer life was peculiar. However, on that evening in 1978, I heard a command and I argued. In fact, I was sure I knew best.

"Not a chance. I'm not going to do it, Lord. They hate me. Why would I help any of them?" I prayed again, sure logic would win out. The request was completely unreasonable. Did I mention those kids did not like me?

"Okay, Lord, you know what's happening at that party, right?"

The argument started again. I probably stomped my foot. After all, my goal was to curl up and read the night away.

But Jesus had not changed His mind or my mission.

"You really want me to drive a bunch of drunken kids home from a wild party?" Unbelievable. "But Lord, you know how I feel about wild parties." A bit of the old fear pelted my imagination. "Lord, I don't understand." With a glance at my fingernail, which still carried a black tip from its run-in with the car door, I remembered, "Let her go. She belongs to Him."

"But, Lord," I reasoned, "that is why I don't think I should have to go."

Since arguing was getting me nowhere, I took the message to my mom, thinking she'd never say yes. She didn't like my old friends.

"Hey, Mom, I've been having an argument with God."

Both eyebrows lifted, and she shook her head. I was such a freak.

"What about?" she asked politely.

"Well, Fred and the gang want me to be the DD tonight. The seniors from school are attending this big kegger. I said no. But when I prayed about it, well. . ." I spit it out. "Jesus wants me to drive. He doesn't care that they hate me."

I looked at my tough, schoolteacher mother and felt my lips curl in a smirk.

Watch this, God. I am a pushover, but wait until You have to deal with her.

Then my mother turned and said the most unbelievable thing. "Jennifer Lynne, if you truly believe Jesus wants you to drive your old friends to this party, you should do it."

Grumbling filled my heart when she returned to her bookkeeping. I felt a little like Jonah when he was told to go to Nineveh. Like him, I wanted to run in the opposite direction.

"Okay, Lord," I said. "I will obey, but I'm not happy about it."

I was on my way to call Fred when the phone rang. Of course it was him.

"Are you sure you can't drive?" he pleaded. "It will ruin our senior party if no one gets to drink. Please, Jennie?"

Consenting grudgingly, I gritted my teeth and told him I'd do it.

Getting ready that night, I caught a glimpse of my finger and stared at the nail. Light pink skin replaced the bruised tissue. About this time last summer, I was getting ready for another kind of party. With thankfulness, I resigned myself to this mission.

When the group picked me up, I got in with the understanding that I'd be given the keys to the car when we arrived. When we turned onto a long, gravel driveway, I saw a long, wood-frame lodge to our right. I promised God I'd stop grumbling then I crawled into the back seat to read. I lost track of time as I turned pages and soon found myself sitting alone in a dark car.

Why hadn't I brought a flashlight? Fear crept into my heart, and I let out a small shriek when I heard tapping against the window.

It was Fred. "I thought you might be bored. Is it okay if I keep you company?"

I consented. And after a few minutes, I learned Fred came to the car alone to find out about Jesus. "I want what you have," he whispered, his voice shaky. "You've changed. It's like someone turned on the lights inside you." Then he admitted, "I'm ready to hear about Jesus."

Fred invited Jesus into his heart, and afterward I told him about my fight with God. I smiled as I told him about the shepherd who left ninety-nine sheep to find the one that was lost. God loved Fred so much that He basically ordered me to come to this stupid kegger. Cool, right?

The party finally came to an end at about one o'clock in the morning. The driver, who I'll call Randy, came out, determined to get behind the wheel after all. He was smashed out of his mind, and the guys wrestled the keys from his grip. Even the really drunk kids didn't want Randy driving them home.

"If he's driving, I'm walking," I said. "I did not come and wait for six hours to die in a crash."

I'd already gotten into one car and regretted it. I had promised myself I would never do that again.

I started walking toward the road. Fred joined me, and the others followed him. Randy watched as we all began to walk away. Finally, he grudgingly agreed to let me drive. He handed me the keys, and seven kids piled into the sedan, one on top of the other.

"Wait," a guy yelled, pounding on the window. I looked up and saw Tres, the local stoner.

"Jennie, take me home, too. I don't have a ride." He appeared scruffy, but I'd always liked him. No one complained when he jumped in, but someone puked. The stench of vomit filled the car, and I gagged. "Roll down the windows!"

I thought about complaining to the Lord, but I was still amazed that Fred had given his heart to Jesus.

At seventeen, I was an inexperienced driver and unaware that even a light rain could cause the road to become slick. We had only been driving for a few minutes when we came to a steep hill. The incline reminded me of a rollercoaster with a row of houses from top to bottom. Protecting those houses was a guardrail, scarred from multiple collisions. Our headlights revealed dents and streaks of car paint. "How many times did a house get hit before they installed a guardrail?" I wondered aloud.

The unmistakable sound of retching was followed by a drawn-out word: "Gross."

Another puker.

At least this guy was next to the door and could hang his head out the window. As the traffic light at the bottom of the hill turned red, I applied the brakes and felt the car begin to shimmy. We slid through the traffic light, and I was grateful there were no cars coming the other way.

"I told you I should be driving," Randy said, slurring his words.

I slammed on the brakes, applying every ounce of pressure my ninety-pound frame could muster, and turned into the skid. We took a collective breath as the car came to a stop, but our relief vanished as a train whistle shattered the stillness. My ears popped as a train thundered past our open windows. The locomotive was only a few feet away from where we sat in our car, listening to the train cars whizzing past.

Ba da bump,

Ba da bump,

Ba da bump.

The car filled with the roar of the train as it rolled by. After our initial screaming terror, relief settled in and we began to laugh. We started counting the cars—sixty-six, sixty-seven. Even when we lost count, I kept thinking, *How long is this train?*

"Wow," someone said from the back seat. "Somebody up there must like us."

I smiled. "You have no idea!" Then the truth dawned on me. "Merciful Father," I whispered, "would they be dead if I hadn't listened?"

With a pounding heart, I watched the train continue on its way before finally disappearing into the night. Putting the car into gear, I crossed the tracks and drove everyone home.

Fred, by the way, became a chaplain in the United States Army.

One week before my wedding, a handsome, clean-cut, young man jumped in front of me at Youngstown State University.

"Jennie Mink. I've been looking for you."

I took a step back. "Who are you?"

"I'm Tres. I changed my name back to Paul." He grinned. "Like Saul, I became Paul. It is really my given name."

He was so excited, and his enthusiasm made me smile. He could see I had no memory of his face. "It's Tres. I sat on your couch on your birthday, and you told me about Jesus, remember? I'm a Christian now."

Recognition dawned, and my mouth dropped open.

"No way!"

"It's true, and I had to find you. I decided to call myself by my given name, Paul. The Tres you knew doesn't exist anymore. Thank you for telling me about Jesus."

We chatted for a bit, but I had to go because of wedding preparations. Once again, I was reminded of the night I had argued with Jesus. Tres was the scruffy, long-haired stoner, the last to jump into the car.

Wow, Lord, two souls for one act of obedience.

Last winter I reconnected with Paul and his lovely wife. He sent me a note: "Hey, Jenn, thanks for driving that night."

Six years after the kegger, I'd nearly forgotten the entire incident. Except for a Christmas card or two, I even lost touch with Fred.

In November of 1984, my husband Bob and I went home for the Boardman High School class reunion. Mom was away, but we stayed at her house in my old bedroom. At about two o'clock in the morning, the phone started ringing. As incessant as an alarm clock, the clanging bell on the old phone pierced my dreams until I realized no one else was going to answer.

I stumbled to my mother's office and put the heavy handset to my ear. "Hello?"

A man's voice replied, "Is this Jennie Mink?"

"The last name is Porter now. But, yes, this is Jennie."

A stream of cussing and cursing made me pull the phone from my ear. What in the. . .

"Who is this?" I asked.

"I'm coming to get you. You ruined my life, and I'm going to ruin yours."

"Who is this? I think you have the wrong number."

"It's Randy."

"I'm sorry, who? I don't think I remember a Randy."

"It's Randy Howard, and I hate your guts." No need to add the unpleasant cussing that followed; you get the picture. I didn't even remember him. He started rambling, and I heard a string of names I did recognize. They were the old friends I had lost when I met Jesus.

Oh, Father. I drew in a quick breath as I remembered Randy Howard.

"Okay, okay, Randy, what is this all about?" I tried to sound calm, but my heart was racing. Putting my hand over the receiver, I called for my husband.

"You ruined my life." It sounded like Randy was crying. "You took away all of my friends with your—your Jesus."

"What could I possibly have done to ruin your life? I haven't seen you in what—six years?"

"Jesus! You had to tell everyone about Jesus!"

I was beginning to wake up. "You've called because of Jesus?"

I couldn't understand everything he was saying amid the cursing and hatred from the other side of the phone until I heard these words: "I hate you. I've always hated you."

I shared the earpiece with Bob.

"They all became Jesus freaks just like you." Randy continued cursing God and me. Then he began to name our old friends one by one. "They all became Jesus freaks—just—like—you!"

As he repeated each of their names, I silently thanked God for each one of them. I was stuck in the moment, totally in awe of my Lord and my King. Wow. God was letting me know that all but one had accepted His Son as Lord and Savior.

My heart twisted with compassion for the angry man on the other side of the phone. "Randy, you can know Jesus, too."

He began to threaten my life.

I handed the phone to my giant husband, a six-foot-four, former offensive tackle for Youngstown State University, and watched as Bob's hazel eyes widened.

"Who is this?" Bob bellowed, his deep baritone echoing in the empty room. "Come here. I dare you. If you come after my wife, you are going to have to fight me first."

The line went dead, and my husband pulled me into his warm, muscular arms. The bully hung up. No surprise. He wasn't so powerful after hearing Bob's booming and, I might add, very protective voice.

So, Lord, when I didn't want to be inconvenienced with people who hated me, You had a plan all along? You protected me at camp, and then, through one act of obedience, You saved an entire car full of kids.

Thank you for sending saints like Mary E. London to guide me in Your ways. Thank you for Linda, who loved me and taught me about You. Each one of those kids saved in the summer of 1978 is a jewel in her crown.

And as for the argument with Jesus, I'm glad I lost that one. By my calculation, God saved eight lives and six souls with one act of reluctant obedience.

And the biggest miracle of all? I became a new creation and learned to listen and obey. God did the rest.

Jennie Porter is a freelance writer and proofreader living in northeastern Ohio. She was a history major, earning a BS in education from Ashland University. Jennie's eclectic experiences include being an in-house writer for Chaparral Christian Church in Scottsdale, Arizona, a soprano vocalist, and a director of drama. She also served as a tutor for Asian graduate students at the Thunderbird School of Global Management in Glendale, Arizona. Jennifer is particularly passionate as a prayer warrior, intercessor, and prayer coordinator.

CHAPTER FIVE

WRITING ON THE WALL
STEVE TAITT

W e've all had that experience. Sometimes we are searching and are still surprised when we find our answer. Other times we are on cruise control and caught completely off guard when God gets our attention.

One Sunday night in Oklahoma City, Oklahoma, I sat in an agony of indecision. That night was just like any other in our small Baptist church, and I was sitting on an oak pew half way back and on the left. Beside me, a red carpet ran down the center aisle and ended at the platform where the empty choir loft rose behind the guest speaker. That preacher was preaching away from the passage where Abraham sent his servant out to seek a wife for Isaac.

Then it happened. Out of nowhere, God seemed to lean over and whisper in my ear, "What about you?"

After that, I only half-listened to the sermon while God and I had a private conversation. Scriptures came to mind, and God's Word spoke directly to me. I turned the words over in my thoughts.

God is the same yesterday, today, and tomorrow. I served the same God who provided signs so that Isaac would get the right wife. So, God, how about You give me a sign so that I can make the right decision? Yes, I know, it's an evil generation that seeks a sign. Yes, we are supposed to listen to that still, small voice inside our hearts. But I can't forget the story of Gideon, in which you made allowances for the weakness of his flesh and did the fleece thing. Twice.

What was my great decision?

A few years earlier, I sensed God was not opening an opportunity for me to be a youth pastor because He wanted me to be a church planter. I shared this with my wife who promptly replied, "When I married you, I agreed to be a youth pastor's wife, not a pastor's wife. That can't be right."

So, I put the idea on the back-burner until God could get us on the same page. We later traveled to Dallas, Texas, to consider an opportunity to be a youth pastor. During that visit with some church people, God helped us to be in agreement, and we looked forward to starting a church. But where?

Oklahoma City had gospel preaching churches within a stone's throw of each other no matter which way you turned. I was convinced God wanted me where evangelical churches were *not* on every street corner. I visited my sister in Aurora, Colorado, and she showed me around in the area. With only five Baptist churches in a city of over 400,000 people, Aurora definitely was not what you'd call over-evangelized. I was beginning to think maybe Aurora was where God wanted us to serve.

Then, through a complicated series of events, I traveled to Middletown, New York. When I first drove into Middletown, I got slammed with a feeling of home. Odd since I had never been there before. Middletown was home to only 40,000 people, but I could see there was a strong need for an evangelical church. Maybe this was where the Lord wanted us to serve.

After praying about both cities, I told my wife I believed the Lord was calling us to Middletown to start a church. "What about Aurora?" she said. "There are so many more people, so isn't the need greater there?"

She wasn't being obstinate—had I said we should go to Aurora, she would have defended Middletown and reminded me that I felt it should be our home.

My mind drifted back to one of the meetings Dr. Jerry Falwell once had with Liberty University's pastoral students—he called us "preacher boys." After graduating from Baptist Bible College in Springfield, Missouri, Dr. Falwell planned to start a church in Atlanta, Georgia. One student asked what he thought might have happened if he had gone to Atlanta instead of remaining where he was.

Dr. Falwell's answer was simple and profound: "God would have built a Thomas Road Baptist Church ministry and Liberty Baptist College in Atlanta," he said. "This is God's work, and He will build His church wherever we serve Him."

Maybe the *where* didn't matter so much. Maybe, but I still had to decide.

So, after weeks of praying and wavering back and forth, I was in church on that Sunday night and sensed God asking, "What about you? Can you trust Me?"

I thought about Gideon and considered setting out my own fleece. I have family back East, and my sister lived in Aurora. "If my sister contacts me," I told the Lord, "then You want me in Aurora. If anyone back East contacts me, then You want me in New York.

"Wait—no, that isn't fair. I have parents and four siblings living in the East. That would be stacking the deck. Ok, Lord, I will pick two specific sisters, Helen and Bobbie. If Bobbie contacts me, that's Your way of telling me we should move to Colorado. If Helen calls or writes, then we're going to New York."

All this happened before the arrival of the Internet, Facebook, instant messaging, cell phones, and texting. Back then, we had only two ways to communicate with faraway family: through the United States mail or long-distance phone calls. (For you millennials, long-distance phone calls are when you call a phone attached to a wall from another phone attached to a wall and hope someone is home. Then you pay your phone company extra money for each minute you talk, unless it's the weekend, which is when you can get a bargain rate.)

We were not a family who indulged in frequent long-distance dialing, so this fleece was more of a challenge than it may seem. Neither sister was likely to contact me.

For the next couple of days, I didn't share the conditions of my fleece with anyone and went about my business. When I got home from work on Wednesday, I had mail—a letter from one of my sisters. Not one out of three sisters, but one of the two I'd mentioned to God. I was so excited to get that letter from Helen that my wife thought I was crazy.

"What is wrong with you?" she asked, staring at me as I grinned at the envelope from West Virginia. "It's only a letter, right?"

How could I explain? It wasn't just a letter from my sister. It seemed to be a letter from God.

I told her about my fleece and about how I made a sort of deal with God on Sunday. I was holding a letter from my sister that was either already in the mail or mailed the day after God and I had had our conversation. "Our God is so amazing," I said. "To think he would do something like this for me. . ."

I was ecstatic over my answered prayer, but my wife didn't share my enthusiasm. With a deadpan expression, she looked at me and said, "So, you want me to move fifteen hundred miles because you got a letter from your sister? I don't think so. You'd better go back to God and ask for something a little more like the handwriting on the wall for my sake."

I exhaled slowly. *Okay Lord, you heard the lady. I'm pretty convinced, but I need something a little more convincing for my other half.*

I spent the next two days at work praying for something "closer to the handwriting on the wall" without having any idea what that might look like. And I couldn't escape a nagging feeling that I was ignoring how God had already spoken to my heart about Middleton. I felt instantly at home there. So, was that God, or was that just my heart?

God, I have no idea what You may do that makes it clearer for my wife, but it is something she needs. I understand because I needed that letter. I trust in Your grace and wisdom.

Two days later, my wife and I went out for dinner. When we returned, my mother-in-law asked, "Steve, is earning ten cents a foot good for drywall?"

She asked because I had spent the last four years learning all aspects of the drywall trade in order to support my family, and she was trying to be helpful. I explained to her that ten cents per foot is a great rate for hanging Sheetrock or finishing, but not for both. In the Oklahoma City area, five and a half cents per square foot was the low side of the average price for either.

"Why do you ask?"

"Well, I walked to the convenient store and purchased a paper to look for a job. I read the paper front to back and laid it aside. But then I felt. . .well, it was like a voice telling me to go through the classified section again. I thought I was being silly since I already went through it, but I read through it again, and this ad jumped out at me. Here, you look at it."

She handed me the newspaper and showed me where she had highlighted an ad in the Friday, November 27, 1987, edition of the *Daily Oklahoman*:

Drywall Finishers
10 cents per ft.
Middletown, NY area.

I blinked at the paper as my blood raced in my veins. Wow. Wow. Wow.

What was an ad for drywall finishers doing in an Oklahoma newspaper? An ad that wanted drywall finishers—which I was— in a town as small as Middletown, New York?

If you are not familiar with the story of Gideon, God called him to service, and he asked God to verify that calling by showering a fleece with morning dew. Not convinced when he found a wet fleece the next morning, Gideon asked God to do it again—but in reverse. God did not chastise him or appear frustrated. He accommodated him.

Just like He did for me.

I turned to my wife and asked, "It's not written on the wall, but will the newspaper suffice? If you want, I can tape it to the wall."

She took the paper and read the ad. Then she left the living room and went upstairs. A minute later, she came back down and asked to see the paper once more. After reading it a second time, she looked at me. "When do we start packing?"

In January, I left for Middletown on a scouting trip and returned in late February, a few weeks before our fourth child arrived. We moved to Middletown in May of 1988 and started

Cornerstone Baptist Church with one family who had been praying for God to send someone to start a church. During the time we were there, hundreds of people came to know Christ as Savior on the church-purchased property.

I never met anyone who moved from Oklahoma to finish drywall in Middletown, New York. But I do know a couple of people who answered that miracle ad.

Steve Taitt, a graduate of Liberty University, has served as a youth pastor, church planter, and evangelist. He is presently ministering as an evangelist through the ministry of Living Grace 1343, which can be accessed via Facebook at https://www.facebook.com/Living-Grace-1343-276864386163314/.

CHAPTER SIX

PURSUED BY GOD
PEGGY PATRICK

I grabbed my coffee-stained mug out of the pile of unwashed dishes and opened the pantry. "We're out of coffee!!" I shouted to no one in particular.

"We're out of milk, too," my twelve-year-old said, munching on dry cereal at the counter.

I swore under my breath as I opened the fridge. *There goes my mother of the year award. I am such a loser.*

"Oh, and the roaches are back," my sixteen-year-old daughter muttered as she wandered by. As if appearing to prove my daughter's point, a small one scurried across the counter to hide beneath an unwashed dish. We couldn't afford an exterminator. We tried to battle them with various pesticides. Amazing we hadn't all been poisoned.

"Well, if someone would wash a dish around here—" I shouted. But my daughter had already vanished into her room.

I grabbed my purse. "I'm running to the store." The kids could live on dry cereal, but I couldn't survive without coffee. I was already sweating profusely as I walked to my car through the unbearably muggy, July, Florida heat. I lived in hell.

The air conditioning in the car was barely working, but it felt better than the fans in our house. Money was tight. We had to choose between food or air conditioning.

My divorce was finalized a few days before. *Worthless. You are absolutely worthless. Two failed marriages. What a joke.*

Sunday was supposed to be my day to relax, not run errands. A day to cuddle up with my husband, who was now cuddling up with a much younger and prettier woman. *Of course he left you. Look at you. Why would anyone love you?*

My world was pretty much zeroed out by the events of the past few months. An ugly breakup followed by bankruptcy. I was practically catatonic. I felt like I was walking through water. The kids were devastated and angry. This was their second time going through this nightmare.

My mother made it clear to me she wasn't going to bail me out of this mess, not this time. Many of my friends, though sympathetic at first, didn't want to deal with my drama. Divorce has a way of making others look at their own relationships and wonder if it could happen to them.

Fat and forty. Guaranteed to be alone forever. Someone once said that at forty, a woman had a better chance of being killed by terrorists than getting married. I had two chances at marriage. Blown them both. And now all I had left were two angry teenagers and loneliness.

Loneliness lived in my chest. Heavy and ponderous. I couldn't breathe. It drained the color out of everything. Everyone else in the world seemed to have a husband or a boyfriend.

I would wake up at night soaked in sweat and gasping for air. My pillow would be stained from tears. I finally reached a point where I didn't have any tears left. I didn't have any feelings left except for a feeling of compete worthlessness. The only reason I didn't kill myself was my kids needed me, poor excuse for a mother though I was.

On my way to the store, I drove by a little church that I had passed many times before. That day, the church sign said, God Loves You. I sat at a stoplight and stared at the sign. I drove past the church and then decided to come back around the block. *God loves me? He'd be the only one.*

I turned into the church parking lot and sat there, frozen. I hadn't been in a church for more than twenty years. I wasn't dressed for church. I had on faded jeans, flip-flops, and a favorite t-shirt emblazoned with "Got a Dime? Call Someone Who Cares." Prior to my divorce, the slogan seemed hilarious. Now it was just true.

I slipped in the back door of the church and slid into a pew. The minister was in mid-sentence. "God loves you," he said, looking straight at me. "God loves you."

I got up, raced back out to my car, and drove to the store. I couldn't stop crying. I couldn't breathe. *God could love me? Me? Hideous, awful, pudgy, unloved, unwanted me?*

A few weeks later, I went back to that church and started going sporadically, mostly for the social connection. I made a few friends, and once a month we got together at someone's house in the evening to talk about life and pray. We sat around on comfy sofas, nibbled on cookies, and chatted about our hopes and dreams. One night after a particularly intense discussion, we settled in for a period of silent prayer.

I leaned back into the couch and closed my eyes.

An unexpected breeze ruffled my hair. Fresh air that was fragrant with flowers. I opened my eyes, surprised by the brilliant daylight all around me. Where was I? Rolling green hills. Vivid. Emerald. Like velvet. Stretching as far as I could see in every direction, stopping only at the edge of a brilliant blue sky.

I looked down at my feet. I was barefoot. The grass was cool and soft. I felt so alive. Was I dreaming? It didn't feel like a dream. It felt real, more real than even. . .reality. I drank in the amazing air and heard a soft cooing sound. Almost a murmur. I saw a bird, bright white against the verdant sod. I spotted another and another until a river of white birds seemed to beckon me across the green landscape. I waded through the birds—doves, I think—my feet luxuriating in the cool grass. They parted for me to walk among them.

I followed the doves until I came to a small hill. I was able to climb it with no effort. As I came over the top, I saw a man in white seated on a rock. The murmuring doves surrounded Him. His long, golden brown hair framed his lovely, gentle face. He seemed to be conversing with the birds. Without being told, I knew He was Jesus Christ.

He stroked one of the doves in His hand. I was so startled to see Him that all I could think to stammer was, "What are you doing here?"

He looked up and smiled. "Waiting for you to get here."

I stood there, motionless. I studied His face. Everything about Him was real, human, and warm. He sat ten feet in front of me. His eyes were so deep, kind, gentle, and beautiful. I took a step forward to see Him more clearly, to look more deeply into His perfect eyes. Somehow, His eyes locked onto mine with the most powerful connection I had ever experienced. Images of everything I was and had ever been flashed through me. Quick images of me with my father, me playing in my grandmother's home, my parents arguing, me screaming at my husband, slamming doors, crying children, my junior prom, pain, loneliness, broken glass, divorce papers. Everything good and bad. Every dark thought, bad word, and stupid action.

But I sensed intense, real, perfect, powerful love layered over all the ugliness. Love in spite of it all. Love unconditional, abundant, and specific. Love of me even though He knew exactly who I really was. He knew everything about me from birth until this moment. He knew my secret dreams and darkest thoughts, yet He still loved me.

His eyes were so powerful and overwhelming that I fell to the ground. I was so unworthy of this love. I had to look away. I wept for all I was, for all I had lost. I wept for my children and failed marriages. I wept because I had never felt love like this from anyone, ever. My body was wracked with sobs as I crawled across the grass to touch His white robe. Such love, such peace swept over me and flooded my heart. Everything I didn't deserve. I pressed the smooth fabric to my tear-stained face and curled up at His feet.

I opened my eyes. My friends in the living room were staring at me as tears streamed down my cheeks.

"What happened?"

"Did you see something?"

"What's wrong?"

I couldn't speak. I couldn't figure out what to tell them. I couldn't explain that I had just met and talked to Jesus Christ. I was still engulfed in the experience.

"I can't talk about this right now, okay?" was all I could whisper. And I didn't talk about it until a few days later when I finally told one friend who kept pressing me for an explanation.

"I saw Jesus Christ."

"You saw Jesus?"

I saw doubt all over his face, so I never talked about it again. But I knew something significant had happened. I just didn't know what. I didn't have any frame of reference for the experience, so I simply tucked it away.

About a month after that, I decided to change my life. I sold my house and all my furniture. I packed up a few boxes and moved my little, single-parent family to Los Angeles, California, to chase my dream of being in the entertainment business. There was nothing left for me in Florida, so why not?

Rolling green hills. Birds. . .

A car horn jarred me out of my daydream. Years had passed since that strange encounter, but it remained with me.

My sleek, blue convertible inched forward in the traffic. Los Angeles traffic was the worst, especially the climb up Coldwater Canyon out of Beverly Hills.

My current car cost more than my Florida house. So much had changed since then. I became a talent and literary agent—a flashy job, offering great money and lots of flashy parties. My clients won Emmys and Oscars. I loved my gorgeous office with its mahogany desk and brocade Queen Anne chair. People complimented my office's view, which included a balcony garden tucked behind French doors. I even had a coveted title: Vice President of Television. Pretty swanky. Best of all, I had married a wonderful, loving man.

My perfectly manicured nails tapped on the steering wheel as my car inched along. I reached into my designer bag to check the time on my cell phone. My purse cost more than the car I drove in Florida. So ironic.

So, if this was success, why did I still have a feeling something was missing? Why did I feel like all of this wasn't enough? That I wasn't enough?

Church fell by the wayside long ago. I was busy and life was hard. And one thing I learned from my earlier life was that it was up to me to make it work. I had to deal with sixteen-hour days. Demanding bosses. Staff meetings so scary that I would get physically sick the night before them. But I gritted my teeth and persevered. I was a success because of me. My efforts. No one else's.

Still, a nagging feeling, a free-floating anxiety persisted. This could all end in a moment. My oldest daughter had just gone through a disastrous divorce. She was in a deep, dangerous depression. My fault. I was her role model. I let both of my children down. All the stuff in the world wouldn't change that fact.

I pulled into the gated garage of our elegant townhouse in Studio City. It had taken me ninety minutes to drive ten miles. I was tired. I lugged my heavy briefcase upstairs. Lots of scripts to read.

"Hi! I'm home!" I dropped my keys onto the antique table in our front hall and walked into the living room. My husband was watching some preacher on Christian television.

"The cable guy didn't come again?"

"Nope, no one here to meet him."

My frustration and tiredness started building inside me. The week before, a torrential rainstorm had knocked out our satellite dish, allowing us to receive only the Christian channels and NASA. Really odd. My only escape from work was mindless TV. But with me at work and my husband dealing with his mother in the hospital, we were stuck with a blue-haired woman weeping about "the

Lord." My church in Florida was not into Bible thumping, so I shuddered at our horrible programming choices.

"How can you watch this crap?" I asked. But I used a stronger word than "crap."

He turned to look at me. "Well, have you ever watched it?"

"I give up." I sank onto the recliner. "Whatever."

This time, maybe out of sheer exhaustion, I watched and listened. Joyce Meyer was preaching. She was funny. Plain-spoken. And her message of a personal relationship with God seeped into my resistant mind. God wasn't an impersonal, floating cloud. He wanted to know us. Me. And even more importantly, He forgave me. I needed forgiveness.

A week later, Joyce Meyer held a conference in Los Angeles. I went. Somewhere in the midst of the music and the message, I found myself walking forward during an altar call. Literally overnight, I became a *Christian*.

What did that mean for me? I started to behave like a Christian. I stopped swearing. We went to church. I read the Bible. I learned about the historical Jesus and began to vaguely understand the theology of His sacrifice for us.

But Jesus was just an idea. A nice idea. A man who taught a great way to live. The Bible had great information in it. But I was still responsible for my life.

A couple of years later, I left my flashy agency job and became a professor at a prestigious Christian university, teaching about screenwriting and the entertainment business. For myself, I took a spiritual formation class where I worked every week with a prayer partner.

I loved those times of prayer. The class was more like a mix of prayer and psychology.

My prayer partner's office, although small, was pretty and serene. The chairs were comfortable, and our time together felt more like friends talking about the deep things of God as opposed to a class. I could tell her anything.

One day she peered at me. "You seem stressed today."

I picked up a pillow and hugged it. "I am. I'm trying to work on some film projects, teach, and take graduate classes."

She took a sip of coffee. "That sounds like a lot."

"It is. And I have a hideous commute, housework, and family stuff. It's like I'm one of those guys in the circus spinning plates. If I pause just for a moment, I'll drop one." I hugged the pillow tighter.

"That makes me stressed just to think about it. Can't your family help?"

"They do what they can, but I'm really the one who makes it happen."

"Well, what about God?"

I suddenly felt uncomfortable in my chair. "What about God?"

"Don't you think you could maybe trust Him with some of these worries?"

I squirmed a bit. "Well, frankly, God has sort of dropped the ball in my life a few times before."

"So, you don't trust Him?"

"I don't know. It just seems like I really have to keep my eye on things because if I don't. . .well, bad things happen."

She set her coffee cup down. "Sounds to me like you might be mad at God."

I was stunned. "I didn't think I was allowed to be mad at God."

"Why not?"

"Because. . .if I do something wrong, won't He take everything away?"

"So, you think you need to be good for Him to love you?"

"That's certainly how it's worked in the rest of my life."

That is what I thought. When I wasn't thin enough, young enough, or pretty enough, I failed at marriage. My children suffered from my bad choices. Where was God for them? I met God one time. I knew He was real. But it certainly seemed to me that He could change His mind at any moment.

My prayer partner smiled. "I think you need to let God know how you feel, how angry you are. Have it out with Him."

I wasn't sure that was a good idea. "How?"

"Read the Psalms. David was very honest with God. God is big enough to handle your anger and disappointment. I don't think you can have a real relationship with Him until you are honest with Him. He already knows what you think."

So, I did, over Christmas break. I journaled. I prayed. I told God about everything He hadn't done to my specifications. I pointed out every place He let me and my children down. I railed against Him.

He listened. I don't know how to explain it, but I felt Him listening. He seemed to be present with me as I wrote and wept. Sometimes, I felt like I understood what happened. Other times, I felt that even though I could never understand it all, He did. And He was still there, loving me.

By the time Christmas break ended, I was eager to get back to my prayer partner. I told her everything, and I told her I felt closer to Him.

"I just wish," I said, sighing, "I could experience Him again. In a real, palpable way."

"You can," she assured me.

"I don't mean in my mind. I mean in a real way."

"You can. You will experience Him as you draw closer."

As I left her office, I found myself praying while I walked across the huge university parking lot. *Please, God. I want to feel You. I want to experience You.*

In that moment, an amazing fragrance wrapped itself around me and stayed with me for a few yards. The embrace of this fragrance mesmerized me. It was heavenly and heady. It brushed past me and then whirled back to caress my cheek and hair. The Holy Spirit wrapped me in a warm hug.

I looked around. I couldn't see any flowers or trees in the vicinity. Nothing but the Spirit of God.

That was the beginning of many more hugs. Standing at the train station in the middle of winter, I inhaled that fragrance, like the lightest touch of a breeze. *I'm here. I love you.* Or on my porch while praying. The fragrance swept down, a whisper of His presence.

I was being courted.

As I advanced in my relationship with the Lord, one of my friends suggested that I meet a wonderful pastor who had planted thousands of churches and was known for his power as a prayer warrior. I had never experienced spiritual warfare. But that evening, as a group of us prayed for the various projects we felt God called us to work on, the strangest thing happened. While the pastor was praying, I began to smell what I thought was a pan burning on the stove. Or maybe a candle gone out. But the odor was so strong that I opened my eyes to see if there was smoke in the room. There wasn't. And there weren't any lit candles.

I looked over to the pastor's wife, thinking she would surely take care of whatever was burning in the kitchen. But she seemed unconcerned. I even thought about stopping the prayer session to warn everyone about a possible fire, but I decided against it since I didn't see any smoke and I didn't want to embarrass our host.

Later, in the car with my friend, I asked, "Did you smell that awful smell?"

"What smell?"

"When we were praying. It was awful. I thought something was burning in the kitchen."

"Peggy, there was no smell."

I stared at her. "Why are you messing with me? Do you have a cold?"

"I have a great sense of smell. But tell me again what it smelled like."

"Like a burnt-out candle or a match after it's been blown out. But a lot stronger."

"Ah." She nodded. "That's the smell of brimstone."

"As in fire and brimstone?"

"Yep."

Spiritual warfare. We were vanquishing the enemy. And for some reason, the Lord let me in on it.

My relationship with this amazing God grew. Lovely, powerful, funny, and delightful. I felt His presence often. When I read the Bible. At night as I drifted off to sleep. During my morning prayer time.

My heart would skip a beat when I sensed His nearness. Praying became something I yearned to do so that I could be near Him. I was falling in love with Him, and He began showering me with little gifts. Everywhere. I called them "God things." They would always show up in places where I couldn't take them back or put them in a lost-and-found. A pearl pendant in the middle of a sidewalk. A diamond promise ring (that fit me perfectly) next to a trash can. A key inscribed with the words "Love never fails" half-buried in the dirt next to my car.

One day, while getting on my train for work, I found another God thing. My station is the first stop for the train, so I am always one of the first people to get on. I liked that because the train was always nice and clean for the day.

While putting my briefcase under the seat, my hand got caught on something, and I pulled out a tiger-eye pendant. Under my seat. I was the only one in the train car. Even the conductor had not been in the car yet.

The most amazing God thing happened on a different day after I had left the train on my way home from work. I was walking through the parking lot when I saw a pile of broken glass on the ground. A shattered bottle. I was about to walk around it, but I noticed one piece seemed out of place, and it was perfectly square.

Now, I am not someone who normally reaches into a pile of broken glass on a whim, but for some reason, I picked up the stone. It was a large, beautifully-cut princess stone, sitting in a pile of broken glass. I took the stone to a jeweler who told me it wasn't a diamond, but he also couldn't tell what it was. "Very curious," he said. I felt sure it was from God.

This season of finding God things lasted about a year, and then it seemed to stop. *Maybe people are being more careful about losing things*, I mused. I, of course, realized these finding incidents might all be coincidences. But each time I found one of those items, I felt like God specifically put it in my path.

Despite all these lovely experiences, I continued to wish I could see Him again. It had been so many years since that first experience, but I thought about it often. *I wish You would come back*, I prayed. *Let me see You.*

Some people I told about the experience scoffed at it. "Why would Jesus Christ personally visit you?" one woman at my church said.

"How did you know it was really Him?" a suspicious seminary professor asked.

I didn't have answers for those questions. Why would He visit me? I am no one, and back then I was less than no one. All I knew was that the love in His eyes and the love that continued to pursue me were real. I also knew that even if I never saw Him again on this side of heaven, I had found a deep and true love in Jesus.

I often found myself praying during my long commutes to and from the university. One evening after an excruciatingly slow drive home, I dragged my heavy briefcase into the house. It had been a long day, but supper and my family were waiting for me. After dinner, I told my husband I needed to go to bed early. Exhausted, I crawled into the cool sheets and felt completely at peace in the quiet room.

I wish I could see You again, Lord. How I love You. Thank you for my life and family. I had changed so much since that first time I met Him.

I was leaning over to turn off the light when I felt the sudden warmth of His presence. The light in the room seemed to change. It softened and became more golden. Then I looked up and saw Him.

Perhaps it was my imagination, perhaps a dream, but Jesus was standing at the foot of the bed with a long-stemmed, red rose.

My heart leapt. He was here! He smiled at me, those beautiful eyes crinkling at the corners. Then He leaned forward to hand me the rose. The fragrance of the flower enveloped me, and I closed my eyes to inhale the scent. When I opened them again, He was gone and so was the rose, but the fragrance remained. And that memory would forever leave an imprint on my heart.

The experience took my breath away. My heart pounded. My King. My Lord. The Love of my life showed Himself to me again. The vividness of the deep red rose overwhelmed me. Red, the color of passion, of love. What did it mean? Somehow, I knew He was showing me that He picked me to be His.

There would be no turning back on this amazing journey toward God.

Peggy Patrick Medberry is a managing partner at Amaris Media International and an associate professor of cinema and media arts at Biola University in La Mirada, California.

CHAPTER SEVEN

WHEN GOD HEALS
SKIP BALL

Lancaster, Lancashire, United Kingdom; 1984

The voice was barely audible but unmistakably His. This time it was filled with urgency.

The old man closed his eyes and furrowed his brow, determined to understand its precise meaning. *Go to Frodsham and visit one of my servants. You must tell him every word I've told you.*

The man scribbled the words on a notepad he kept beside his Bible. On a fresh sheet of paper, his shaky hand rewrote the message word for word.

"I've got to find Frodsham on a map." He spoke to no one in particular. The elderly Mr. Metcalfe lived alone but never far from his adult children. He was quite independent for his age and zealous to listen to God's word, not man's. This evening he had fallen half-asleep with the Bible open on his lap when he heard His voice. Metcalfe sat up straight as he realized the gravity of his mission.

Something was happening in the spiritual realm, and he must alert those on the front line. He reread the text.

Metcalfe's Bible was well worn, torn, and marked. It was used as a roadmap for his entire life, and it never failed him. Psalm 145 was open. With a red pencil, he marked verse seventeen before he dozed. "The Lord is righteous in all his ways and faithful in all he does" (NIV). The next morning, he obtained the pastor's phone number from someone in his own fellowship and made the call.

Frodsham, Cheshire, United Kingdom

I heard the phone ring downstairs. My desk was cluttered with notes, commentaries, and my Bible as I worked on a message in our bedroom. My wife, Lin, called up to me, "Skip, there's a man calling from Lancaster. His name is Metcalfe. He says it's urgent and he must speak with you."

"Thanks, Lin. I'll be right down." Urgent? I couldn't imagine what was so important—and from Lancaster. I hurried down the steps two at a time. His name was faintly familiar.

"Hello, this is Pastor Ball."

He explained that we'd met years earlier and that God recently spoke and told him a great deal about our story. He spoke as if he were reading about us in a newspaper. Metcalfe planned to drive down to pay a visit. Today! He lived seventy miles northwest and would arrive in three hours depending on the traffic. I was dumbstruck. Apparently, it hadn't occurred to him that I might have other plans for the day.

I didn't know anyone who could hear from God like Mr. Metcalfe. How could he know so many details? At first I wondered if he was one of these super religious Christians who had a word from the Lord for everyone. But he'd already confirmed things he couldn't have known otherwise.

I walked into the kitchen and turned on the electric kettle. "Lin, I need to tell you about this phone call." She was busy cleaning around the stove. "Can you sit down a minute? You need to listen to what I've just heard."

"Sure, love. It's got me curious. Who was that man?" She poured steaming tea into two mugs and sat at the table. "His name doesn't sound familiar."

"I know. But I faintly remember two sisters who lived in Lancaster and worked with the teens at the Heysham church. This is their father. He's on his way now. He says he has a message from the Lord and wanted to share it in person." I cupped my hands around the hot mug. "Lin, he told me about us. God is paying attention."

"What do you mean, about us?"

"He shared enough for me to realize he knows a lot about what's happening to us. He even described the threats, harassment, and what this man is doing to us—to you, me, and the kids."

Tears pooled in Lin's eyes. For years we had begged God to send help, to give us some support. We needed some answers. Why was this happening to us? We felt we weren't going to survive.

Mr. Metcalfe arrived at 1:30 p.m. "Bless you both, Pastor and Mrs. Ball. I'm sorry for taking so long. There was heavy traffic, and I probably drive slower than you young people these days."

"Please, come in. Welcome to Erindale Cottage." I faintly remembered him. "Am I right in remembering you have two daughters who worked with the teens in the Heysham church?"

"Yes, you're correct. They believe that's their calling in life."

Lin prepared a fresh pot of tea, some sandwiches, cakes, and biscuits. The three of us sat, and we chatted about church and family.

Mr. Metcalfe wore a woolen, tweed jacket with a white-collared shirt and khaki tie. Layered beneath was a hand-knitted, sleeveless vest for warmth. His thick, wavy hair was pure white. His humble appearance, a Lancashire farmer who spoke few words but with depth of knowledge, invoked genuine confidence. Metcalfe's words and understanding separated him from the average man on the street. We sat together in silence for a while, waiting for him to explain why he came. He closed his eyes for a minute and then offered a prayer.

"God knows you both are His faithful servants. You're building the Kingdom of God in Cheshire. He has placed you on the front line of a very dark battle. As you know, there's always casualties in battle, and you are this man's target. He's terrorizing your family." He paused. "No matter who we are or how strong our stamina, our mind, body, and psyche react differently to abnormal violence. There is no normal response to abnormal behavior." His deep blue eyes studied us intently. "We are created in God's image, but our minds and bodies are fragile and can break when evil men do abnormal things to us. The mind can only cope with so much before it shuts down to protect us from long-term damage."

He was right. Both of us had developed a sense of guilt that we couldn't handle these attacks without crumbling. I chastised myself for letting panic attacks take over. I didn't understand them, neither did my doctor. Lin was suffering from anxiety and severe depression. When the enemy struck, she got hysterical. What woman wouldn't?

God sent Mr. Metcalfe, whom we hardly knew, to calm our hearts and teach us to trust God in the dark times. This man was an expression of God's love to us. We would hold onto this moment when future attacks came. None of this surprised God. Yet, what was coming in the future? What was this terrorist planning, and why us? Why wouldn't God stop it all?

Metcalfe warned, "Our minds and bodies are not designed to withstand such constant, unpredictable attacks. Many soldiers come home from war suffering from PTSD. We must not be ashamed when our minds react to abnormal attacks. God understands, and He wants us to rest in Him."

As quickly as Mr. Metcalfe announced his coming, he stood, ready to leave. "Pastor, I want to pray over you and your wife. You are God's servants. And regardless of what happens, God has told me He will walk with you through the fire. He promises that. You've been through many storms and it's not over yet. More is coming. You're following in the footsteps of our Messiah who suffered for the sins of us all. This might never end. Hold on to God as He holds on to you."

He put both hands on our heads and prayed softly, entrusting us and our children's lives into God's care. And then he was gone. That was the last time we ever saw him.

Vale Royal District Courtroom, Winsford, Cheshire; May 11, 1988

Lin and I anticipated the court date in Winsford. It was a day mixed with both dread and hope. We prayed and trusted God for victory. Unfortunately, it was our last stand to find justice for our family. Mr. Johns was finally arrested. After years of terror, he was caught in the act. His reign of terror stopped for one night. Someone paid his bail. At two o'clock in the morning, after all the pubs were closed, he was released and set free to harass us with threatening phone calls. That brief respite gave us hope that the courts would find a just response to his crimes against us and against God. For that brief spell, our spirits lifted.

My wife and I walked out of the Vale Royal district courthouse, shocked beyond belief. The courts were not favorable toward our case. Outside, the sky was threatening all morning, but suddenly the heavens burst open in a rage. A couple from church drove us there, anticipating how difficult the trial might be. Our doctor gave Lin a short prescription of beta blockers to help her stay in control when she was interrogated by the man who'd been trying to destroy our lives. Lin could not look him in the eyes. His smirk and cocky swagger made it hard to have any respect for him. Yet, the courts allowed him to represent himself. Of course, no local attorney would take his case.

This was a magistrate's court with three judges, two of whom were lay judges from the local community with no legal qualifications. They could be anyone in the village. We had hired our friend Mr. Harmond, a Christian brother and our property solicitor. He had helped us with the purchase of our house. He knew the basic laws of courtroom procedure, but this defendant was a wild card. No one wanted to go against him.

We had one primary witness, the arresting officer who had found the weapon in the defendant's hand, a long-handled sledgehammer that was used to terrorize us by pounding our living room wall for nearly half an hour before he was arrested. He damaged a large section of our wall. The children were terrified. He weakened the wall, causing the bricks to crumble on both sides. It was in danger of collapsing.

Mr. Harmond was articulate and presented a clear case against the defendant, Mr. Noel Johns. Trying to convict a man with a mind bent on destruction was not something Harmond had done before. Today, the only charge against Mr. Johns was the most recent attack. As far as the courts were concerned, we couldn't speak of the personal threats or the numerous attempts he had made against our lives over the past several years. Mr. Harmond looked distressed. He called his key witness.

"I call Constable Mercer to the witness stand." Solicitor Harmond asked the witness to describe what he found when he first arrived at Erindale Cottage on the night in question.

"I found the defendant, Mr. Noel Johns, holding a sledgehammer, Exhibit A, in his hands."

"And what was he doing with the sledgehammer?"

"He was swinging it against the exterior of their living room wall as if he were at a demolition site."

"Speculation," the defendant shouted.

"I withdraw that statement." Mercer cleared his throat. "When I asked him to stop, he ignored me. He kept screaming curses as he swung away at the wall."

"How did you restrain the defendant? Did he cooperate?"

"It took myself and Constable Jones to restrain him. Finally, I tackled him. He dropped the weapon, and I kicked it away from his reach. He fought until I cuffed him and put him in the squad car."

"What damage had been done by the time you came on the scene?"

"He'd loosened the brickwork covering about a six-foot section from top to bottom and approximately four feet wide. Inside, the wall had started to crumble." Mercer added, "It seemed as if he were trying to break into the house."

The defendant jumped to his feet and shouted. "Hey, hey, you. No one asked for your opinion. You have no idea what was in my head!"

The judge hit the gavel. "Order, order in the court. Mr. Johns, you've requested to defend yourself. Therefore, you must follow court procedure. No more outbursts like that."

By the time it came for cross-examination, Johns's tone had become sly and cunning. He grilled Lin by getting in her face, intimidating her with stares and sarcasm. Somehow, he managed to control the entire courtroom.

An hour later, all charges against him were dismissed. Lin and I looked at each other in total disbelief. There was no justice for our cause. I held Lin's hand and could feel the tremor running up her arms. She was crying. Johns was smirking. He looked at us and grinned.

"Mr. Noel Johns, you are free to go."

He walked out of the courtroom a free man, laughing all the way.

As we exited the courtroom, Officer Mercer caught up with me. "Sir, I've been an officer for eight years, and I can't believe this has happened. How did he get away with all those crimes? He made a mockery of our judicial system." He shook his head in disbelief. "I caught Mr. Johns committing a criminal act with the weapon in his hands. I saw him hit the wall. How could they ignore that, including the photos of damage to your home?" He was angry. "I'm sorry, but I can't understand how this case could be so easily dismissed. Pastor, I've been called to your home on numerous occasions when Johns was terrorizing your family. I've seen your children crying and your wife hysterical, rightly so." His fists clenched. "He should be behind bars."

"Thank you for believing in us. God is our helper. May He bless you for standing with us at this critical hour." We shook hands. "God is our judge and His judgment is perfect. We need strength to hold on through this ordeal."

"I was certain we'd win this case," Mercer went on. "In a magistrate court, the three judges must be unanimous, or the case is dismissed." He started to leave then paused. "Of all the cases in which I've been called as a witness, your case was one of the clearest because it was simple and straightforward. Mr. Johns had nothing, nothing at all." He shook his head in dismay. "So much for British justice. That's all I can say." Mercer gave one last nod and walked toward his car. I heard his loud mufflers as he roared away from the car park and sped out of sight.

Neither of us had any experience with courtroom drama, here or back in the States. I assumed the facts would speak for themselves in any democratic society. Something wasn't right, but we didn't have the energy or money to fight this case. I would have to pay for all the damages, and we would have to move on with our lives. No matter what the outcome was today, I knew full well, from his own words, that Mr. Johns hated the God we worshipped, and as long as we lived in this town we were his enemy. God was on trial here.

On that day, we felt only defeat. Lin and I were no longer able to lift the other. We both withdrew into our own circle of pain. Mine was a constant petition, desperate for answers.

God, I can't hear your voice. You know how I've agonized over this harassment for so long. Now the decision has been made. Lord, for whatever reason, You allowed this guy to walk! How do we live with this? What do we do now? Where do we go to be safe? He'll probably be home before we get there. I can't take the chance of him doing something to my family. There's no way I'll let my wife and children go back into that house, not at least until we have another plan. And all my plans have failed. God, where are You? Please, God, I need to hear your voice!

We deliberately kept the court hearing from the congregation as much as possible. We were grateful that key church leaders and my superintendent were there. God was there, but I didn't feel Him. My head was screaming for help, but the silence was deafening.

Lin was so overwrought that she struggled to walk down the courthouse steps in the rain. I held her arm, guided her into the back seat of the car, and climbed in after her. She was inconsolable. She was subpoenaed as a witness. I worried for her mental health. During the cross-examination, Mr. Johns paraded back and forth, asking questions that seemed inappropriate, attempting to make her look foolish.

Because I was at church the night of the crime, I was not allowed to testify. It tore me up to watch her take the stand alone and not be able to come to her defense. The defendant finally reduced her to tears on the witness stand.

We'd had enough.

Our friends, Peter and Pauline, were stunned into silence. They drove us because of just this possibility. I'd claimed so many verses, prayed with other pastors, pleaded with God over these years. I had looked for another place to rent and tried to sell the house. What more could we have done? The scenes that played out in the courtroom were a total joke, and we were stunned beyond belief.

Erindale Cottage, Frodsham

Peter Gates took Lin and our boys to the home he shared with his wife, Pauline, then he took me home. Our house was dark and foreboding. Just around the corner was the man who had won. I lit the gas fire, fixed a cup of coffee, and sat with only the fire for light. Johns had skulked around our house in the dark for so long that we were paranoid.

I closed my eyes and wept. My body longed for sleep, but my mind was a whirlwind—nightmares came unbidden. The story of our relationship with Johns was long and filled with hatred.

The trouble began in the early part of September 1984. The estate agency Entwistle Green sent one of its representatives over with mortgage documents for us to sign. I experienced that magic moment when I finally held a handful of ancient keys to our first home, a century-old chauffeur's cottage, derelict and unlivable. I was given six months to make it habitable, or we would lose the deposit, and the contract would be null and void.

It was dark when I pulled up to the cottage. With a flashlight in my hand, I tried every key until one worked. With our ministry well established, I was eager to have a home of our own. Lin was willing to trust me. It took muscle to unlock the door and shove it open. Inside, the place reeked of cat urine. The door closed behind me, leaving me in the dark.

I clicked on my flashlight. From out of nowhere, someone began kicking and beating the door as he screamed and cursed. I had no idea who he was. I'd never met him before or had any knowledge of him.

"I'm going to destroy you and your family," he shrieked outside the door. "I know who you are, and we'll see what your little God can do to stop me. You'll never succeed."

I pulled the door open and Johns lunged toward me. "I hate you, and I hate your God."

Blinking, I stood face to face with the man who would become my nemesis. Because his hatred was so intense toward a person he'd never met, I understood hatred against God drove his rage. Jesus warned His disciples, "If the world hates you, keep in mind that it hated me first" (John 15:18, NIV). I wondered who had hurt him—his father, a priest, the war?

After telling my wife about the encounter, Lin and I were determined to love him and his family with Christ's love. That was the first day of a five-year war that nearly tore our family to shreds.

Johns's threats were genuine. He had a propensity to create chaos toward our children, my wife, and our church family. He destroyed one of our son's birthday parties by setting off fire crackers beneath cars as the children played nearby on the lawn. Everyone fled. He sent news reporters from a London tabloid to our home to interrogate us, claiming we were some Jim Jones cult. Attacks came like darts from every direction. He kept us off guard by switching tactics so that we never knew when or where the next attack would come. We soon were living in dread.

One Easter Sunday, we came home to find flames shooting out of our chimney and our house filled with soot and smoke. He'd lit a fire by knocking a hole into the exterior chimney wall. He found great pleasure in humiliating us in town, ramming our car or chasing us through the streets.

The attacks grew steadily worse and more deviant in nature. One night, I caught him on a ladder outside our sons' bedroom window. He lunged at them from the window, tormenting them in the semi-darkness. Then, after nine months of us feeling nauseous and the children struggling to breathe, we discovered he had pumped carbon monoxide into our home through a vent. The invisible fumes sent two of our sons to the hospital.

From that time on, we moved all our beds into one room and camped together. I put our names on a housing list for rentals. The wait, we were told, could last up to two years. Meanwhile, the church was exploding with conversions of entire families as teens, parents, and grandparents came to Christ.

Lin and I tried to carry the burden of harassment quietly, telling only a few church leaders. But eventually our young believers realized something was wrong. They saw the stress and anxiety on our faces. One day, I collapsed in the street from a severe panic attack. As the church continued to grow, we found momentary strength to fight against revenge and hatred, but something had to change.

Five years later, at the courthouse, the day began with hope for justice and ended with defeat. We were spent, numb, and unable to think of a way ahead.

God, where is justice for our family? Where is the support we need?

I pled with my superiors for a sabbatical, but for logistical reasons, they had to deny my request. We felt alone and abandoned. We were raising three young sons and ministering to the community through a vibrant church in this village. Despite our personal terror, God placed His hand of protection over the new believers. God was at work in Frodsham.

We were left in a quandary. How does one walk away from his calling because of one man's hatred against Jesus Christ? We looked at every logical option and came up with nothing. Lin and I pled with God. We prayed for answers and tried to find a way to live through the terror.

Of course, God was listening. He always does.

And He had ways of letting us know He was watching. June, an elderly woman in our fellowship, prayed and waited for twenty-five years for a church to be birthed in Frodsham. She cast her lot with us the day we began our ministry. She knew the terror we were facing. One windy day, as she was busy hanging out her laundry, something startled her. The sky grew brighter until the clouds became brilliant white. June forgot her laundry and watched in amazement. Bright beings were gathering. They joined hands and hovered over a little, dark house, Erindale Cottage. They prayed against the encroaching darkness and for the protection of the family inside as evil repeatedly attacked.

June had rarely seen a vision. But as the sky faded back into England's blustery weather, she knew God's hand was upon the pastor and his family. She dropped the clothespins into the basket and rushed to call me.

When we got the call, Lin and I praised and thanked the God of heaven for assuring us He was watching every heartache and hearing every prayer. His eyes were upon us whether we felt Him or not. This was spiritual warfare, and God's warriors were surrounding us.

But after that court date, all appeared lost. We had no place to go where we'd be safe.

Just before nightfall, the clouds lifted to reveal the last of the setting sun. But by nine o'clock in the evening, rain pelted, bringing with it a howling wind. I called Lin to make sure she and the lads were okay. There wasn't much to say. Our world was so dark and heavy.

"Lin, I love you so much. When the lads wake, tell them Dad loves them. Make sure Chris takes his meds and his inhaler. Did you pack one with him? Tell Danny he's my boy. Give Jonny a big squish for me. Give them all hugs." I felt loss so deeply and a sudden fear overcame my thoughts. "Lin, if you or the kids need me, call, please. Promise? Just call me. I'll come over right away. I miss you, babe."

"Skip, we're okay," she assured me. "Pauline has fixed the room up nice for us. There's two sleeping bags on the floor, and Jonny is sleeping in the bed with me. We're fine." Lin took sleeping medication. She was groggy.

"You haven't told them anything, have you?" I asked.

"Of course I haven't. All they would understand is that the evil man is not going to be locked up for his crimes. I'll let you figure out what to say." After a pause, she said she was going to bed. "Let's talk in the morning. We've got to decide what we're going to do. Goodnight, Skip."

"I love you, Lin." But she'd already hung up.

I felt isolated from my family. The house grew cold. Our cottage was surrounded by the National Trust forests, and tonight the rain on the trees seemed to clatter louder than on a tin roof. The world outside seemed blacker than it ought to be.

A chill ran down my spine that wasn't from the cold—it was much deeper. Evil won. . .this round. The gloom of the night seemed to press against the windows, suck the air out of the room, and constrict my breathing. Where are You, God? Don't abandon us. I've given my life to serve You.

I finally fell asleep somewhere in the midst of the darkness. My dreams brought the face of a laughing man. He cackled and cursed, "Your God is too small." The face taunted, "I hate your God!" An image emerged of a shadowy figure who held a sledgehammer. It came down, and I jolted up in bed.

I reached over and turned on my bed lamp. I was sweating, yet the room was cold. My sheets were tossed on the floor. I'd been wrestling. The words of Metcalfe came back to me: "There's more to come. . .but God is with us."

Dread took up residence next to me in the bed. I grabbed my Bible and turned to Isaiah 43:1–3. No dreams, voices, threats, or courts could rob me of the God I serve.

I paced the room and read aloud: "Do not fear, for I have redeemed you; I have summoned you by name; you are mine. When you pass through the waters, I will be with you; and when you pass through the rivers, they will not sweep over you. When you walk through the fire, you will not be burned; the flames will not set you ablaze. For I am the Lord your God, the Holy One of Israel, your Savior" (NIV). Those promises were for God's people who went through floods, fire, and storms. He went through them with us. Apparently, He didn't decide to remove them, but He would always be there.

I slept. At six o'clock in the morning, I thought I heard the phone ring. Then it stopped. I dozed off. When I awoke, I was in too much turmoil to stay in bed. Downstairs, the phone rang again. By the time I got to it, it stopped ringing.

I turned on the gas fire but still felt chilled. I went back upstairs and dressed in warm clothes then went down. I dozed on the sofa for a few minutes only to wake feeling as if someone was in the room.

I prayed in a loud voice, angry at Satan's tactics. "In the name of Jesus Christ, Lord of all, I command you, Satan, to get out of this house, out of our family's lives, and out of the church. We have claimed the town of Frodsham for the Kingdom of God, and your tricks cannot stop us."

I went into the kitchen and turned on the electric kettle. After fixing a cup of tea, I sat at the kitchen table, staring at nothing. My mind was reeling. I felt confused and my heart began to race, but I kept holding onto God.

"Lord," I prayed, "I've tried to remain faithful through these difficult years. This man has tested my patience, and he's gotten the best of me. He's not a phantom—he's real. But now I don't know what's going to happen. How can we live next door to this madman any longer? The children are terrified. Lord, You seem to bless this church beyond anything I imagined. So why can't our lives be fixed?"

A faint voice echoed in my thoughts: *I sent you a man to prepare you for this trial. My guardians are watching over you, night and day. I know it's terrifying, but remember I am with you even in your distress. You're in a war, but I'll be with you to the end. I'll never leave you or forsake you. I want you to keep trusting Me through the fire and the storm.*

In the midst of terror, I rested in His still, small voice. By seven o'clock in the morning, the phone rang again. I suddenly realized it could have been Lin all this time. How foolish of me. I grabbed it. "Lin, I'm here."

"Sorry, pastor, this is Rainy. I'm sorry to call you at this time of the morning. And I know you're under a lot of stress, but Steve's father, Kenneth Powell, is dying. Please, we need your help." Rainy was a fast talker and didn't wait for me to comment. "He and Edna have been attending church. They bring young Michael." She paused. "You know Steve is my brother-in-law.. . .We're all worried sick. Ken had a massive heart attack on May ninth and is now on life support. He's not responding to any treatment—he's in a coma. I'm not asking you to visit, but we felt we had to call you because we don't know if he is right with God. He's at Halton General

Hospital in Runcorn, just in case. He was admitted to Ward B4, but they've had to move him to the ICU."

I mumbled, "I'm so sorry, Rainy. I'll be praying." That old familiar panic began to tighten my throat. I couldn't let anyone see me like this. I had nothing to offer. Nothing!

"If there's anything else you can do, the family would be so grateful," Rainy went on. "You've got the answers, and we want to know he's saved before he dies. That's all. There's nothing more we can do. We're out of options."

"I—I don't—don't think I'll be any help." I was shocked to hear myself stutter. I paused and finally sighed. "I'll go, Rainy. Please tell Steve I'm coming."

I argued with God. I shouted. "I can't do this. I have nothing left in me. I'm a basket case. God, You are asking me to minister to someone else when I can't."

But I had to go. It was my responsibility. But if my faith was powerless to make a shred of difference for my family, how in the world could I call on God for Kenneth Powell? I had nothing to say. My words would only be words. I really didn't know Ken enough to pray for personal matters. He was quiet. He didn't attend church every week. He was a nice enough guy but with a British reserve. I argued with God for half an hour.

By nine o'clock in the morning, I'd taken a shower, shaved, and cut myself twice. I still didn't think I could face anyone. But simple obedience pushed me to respond. What choice did I have? I put on my clerical collar and felt like a phony. Rainy hadn't asked me to go, but the family needed someone there. They needed a pastor. That was me.

I drove through Frodsham, passed over the swing bridge, and headed toward Runcorn, a blue-collar township in the Borough of Halton in Cheshire. The skies were mottled gray, and a heavy mist made it difficult to drive. I began to feel nauseous, one of the first signs of a panic attack. My sight blurred with dark blotches in my vision. My breathing became shallow and fast, and my head began to spin. *I've gotta stop—gotta stop. I'm gonna crash. Jesus, help me.*

I swerved wildly and nearly hit an oncoming car. Several horns honked at me, increasing the chaos and confusion in my head. I jerked the steering wheel to the side and slammed on my brakes, my tires screeching over gravel. I realized I had gone temporarily blind. I was going to pass out.

Breathe slowly, slowly. Close your eyes.

Five minutes later, I lifted my head from the steering wheel. I don't know what happened, but my vision cleared. "Thank you, Jesus." I sat for ten minutes. Slowly, I pulled onto the road again and headed cautiously toward Halton General Hospital.

As I drove into the parking lot, I said, "Lord, I'm supposed to pray for a man who's in a coma. He won't even know I'm there. He's as much as dead. I'm an empty vessel. What can I offer? Nothing! It's up to You."

I met Steve Powell on the front steps of the hospital. The mist stopped, and he had stepped out to get some air. He smiled weakly and we shook hands.

"Hi, Steve," I began. "I'm so sorry to hear about your dad. Rainy called me earlier. I felt I should come. What does the doctor say?"

"He's tried to prepare us for the worst." Later Steve told me the full diagnosis of his father's condition. "My father's physician is Dr. John Williams. He said he's withdrawn all active treatment because he's deteriorated so much. They put him on life support because he couldn't breathe on his own." Steve shuddered and wrapped his arms around himself. "It's been so hard to listen and watch him try to breathe. He also said that my dad developed terminal respiratory secretions. That's where saliva and bronchial fluids fill his throat and upper chest because he can't swallow. They call it the death rattle. It sounds terrible."

We walked through the doors and down the corridor toward Medical Ward B4. I didn't feel like chatting, but Steve needed to talk. He'd been there for four days and was exhausted.

"Has your dad had a history of heart problems?"

"Never. Unfortunately, my dad was on his own when the heart attack happened. That was unusual, but my mum had gone out of town for a few days. My dad was probably enjoying a game of football or cricket on the telly when the attack hit him. Somehow, he managed to crawl to the phone and ring me. My wife, Jackie, and I were together, so she called for an ambulance while I raced to the house. By the time I got there, he was lying on the floor, curled into a fetal position. He was in agonizing pain and moaning. I didn't know what to do except talk to him, calm him down, and tell him someone was on the way."

Steve whispered, "It seemed like forever. But eventually the local doctor arrived and gave him a shot of morphine that eased his pain until the ambulance pulled up and began preparing him to head to the hospital."

"Of all the days for this to happen, why did it have to be on his sixty-ninth birthday?" Steve's eyes brimmed with tears that refused to fall. "Imagine, it happened on his birthday." He tried to regain his composure. "I'm sorry for getting upset. I'm just exhausted. I've stood watch every day, hoping to see improvement. But instead, each day he looks worse. His doctor says he's dying."

We walked into the ICU where Ken lay still and silent. He'd been in a coma for four days. Seeing Ken lying there so close to death, not knowing if he'd ever made a confession of faith in Jesus Christ, I felt a pang of guilt for my hesitation. Yet, what could I offer now? I saw no sign of hope for Kenneth Powell.

The sick man lay in a deathlike state—his breath, dead air; his mind, lost in a web of unconsciousness. Enshrouded by monitors and wires, Ken breathed automatically—a clicking sound followed by a rasping, mechanical gasp. Without the ventilator, he would die. A man was being sucked into a world from which he could not return, and no one knew the state of his eternal soul.

I touched his pasty hand. Dark veins protruded like a three-dimensional road map.

As a pastor, I had no right to offer misguided hope for a man whose son hoped against all hope that his father's life would be spared. Where was Ken at this moment? His breathing, the pumping of his heart, the flow of his blood were purely mechanical motions set in place by a machine. A priest would have offered the Last Rites to this dying man. If I were a Jew, this time between life and death would be considered highly sacred. But not to me. I knew of no verse in Scripture supporting that belief. And this modern machine kept Ken's body warm, but where was his soul at this moment?

"Pastor, will you offer a prayer for my dad?"

I nodded, knowing I had no special power or words to change Ken's future. "Of course." Struggling with my own spiritual impotence, I opened my mouth. But the words from my lips did not originate from my mind or heart.

"Lord, raise this man to life. . ." Instantly, I pulled my hand away.

What had I done? I'd just violated an essential principle that I practiced throughout my ministry: give wise counsel and don't offer false hope to broken hearts. I began to tremble. God hadn't told me anything. In fact, I hadn't heard His voice in a long time. That prayer came from my lips but was spoken from beyond my spirit.

The words challenged death and called forth life. I shuddered. I would not own the prayer. I could not.

The monitor on the ventilator began flashing. A nurse hurried in and checked the read-outs. She wrote something on his chart and left. I couldn't read her facial expressions.

A man in a suit waited silently in the doorway. He leaned against the door frame but said nothing. No doubt he had heard my foolish prayer. Cramped in this small room, all I had to offer was empty words. Claustrophobia began to make me sweat. My hands trembled as soon as I walked into this tiny room with a dying body, his son, and this machine.

"Steve, God's love never fails. I'll come by tomorrow morning to see how your dad's doing. Is that okay?"

Steve nodded. He stood there pale and uncertain. Was he expecting a miracle? Obviously, there wouldn't be one. I wanted to console him, to offer hope.

Lord, help me. I can't even think of a single encouraging Scripture.

I noticed the man in the suit was still there. I whispered to Steve, "Is he part of the hospital?"

"Yes, that's Mr. Geoff Hutchinson. He's the consultant surgeon for Halton General Hospital."

"You mean *doctor*?"

"No. Mr. Hutchinson." Steve explained that in the United Kingdom, surgeons are awarded the title "Mister" when they pass the Royal College exams. It's considered a badge of honor.

"He's been very kind to our family. I think he's monitoring my dad's care. He's responsible for the surgical ward. He probably monitors everything that goes on here." Steve paused then said, "I've been told my dad probably won't survive. At some point, they'll disconnect the ventilator and discontinue all treatment. Dr. Williams said they'll let him die naturally." He choked up.

I put my hand on his shoulder. "This must be the worst time of your life."

Feeling I was getting in the way, I stepped through the doorway as two nurses in white uniforms rushed in. At the other end of the hallway, a siren blared as an ambulance pulled up to the emergency entrance. The flashing blue lights bounced off the walls, slid across the floor, and brushed my shoes. Ken's room became a flurry as the nurses wheeled in a gurney and positioned it beside the ventilator. A staff nurse had already disconnected the tubes and wires from his body. All human effort to save Ken's life was exhausted, and he was now in the hands of God.

I concluded the nursing team had disconnected Ken so he could die quietly.

Another pang of guilt stabbed me in the gut. I should have done more. What was my purpose in coming here? I failed to console, offered no biblical inspiration, gave no emotional support, and offered a false hope. God forgive me!

A numbing grief hit me as I watched the three women gently slide the limp body away from the machine and onto the gurney. They placed a pale green blanket around Ken and quickly rolled him out of the room.

As Ken left, paramedics pushed a gurney through the doors and rushed past me. Their patient was a teenage boy, somebody's son, his face torn open with lacerations. Probably a car accident. His left hand dangled over the edge of the bed, leaving a trail of blood along the shiny, tiled floor.

I began to feel a growing panic and an urge to run.

A nurse spoke to Steve. "We'll make your father as comfortable as possible. We're moving him to another ward. You can follow me."

I said goodbye to Steve as he walked behind the nurses. "I'll see you tomorrow."

I was anxious to get away before I had another full-blown panic attack or something worse. My chatter was an attempt to focus on something else until I could slip away.

The surgical ward suddenly got busy, and Mr. Hutchinson rushed off to assist another patient. In the distance, the sound of sirens wailed louder.

I hurried out into a drizzling rain and made my way to the car. My heart was heavy. I had failed the God I love. I had failed everyone. As I turned on the ignition, a rush of warm air steamed up my windows, enclosing me in a cocoon. Using my hand to wipe away the condensation, I smeared the windshield uselessly, making a mess. I drove carelessly through the streets. I yanked off my clerical collar and threw it onto the passenger seat.

My faltering prayer for a son's dad seemed as pathetic as my prayers for my own family. Was my faith impotent? Did my personal quandary prevent me from believing for others? Was ministry allowed only for the servants who were blessed with daily success?

I dreaded the thought of going back to the hospital, but I had promised Steve. Meanwhile, the weight of loss and disappointment left my family and me open to fear and defeat. That night, I called Lin and told her about the Powell family. I talked to the children, pretending everything was good. They were enjoying playing with Peter's big, black Labradors. I didn't tell Lin about my panic attack.

The following morning, I startled awake as the alarm went off. I sat up in bed with a feeling of dread in my stomach. The thought of breakfast made me feel nauseous. I had no idea what to do for our family, but we couldn't keep living like this. I felt that my life was out of control. I didn't want my neighbors, church fellowship, and friends to see what was happening to me. I showered, dressed, and headed back to the hospital under the shadow of an overwhelming emptiness.

As I entered the hospital, a pervasive antiseptic scent mingled with the lingering smells of an institutional breakfast. I walked through Ward B4, heading to the ICU room. A new patient was wired up to the ventilator where Ken had been just hours before. I didn't know where to find him. Walking back through the ward, I scanned the patients' faces. Recognizing no one who looked remotely like Ken, I turned away and grieved for Steve.

Ken probably died within minutes of my leaving the day before. Where was Steve? I needed to contact him. I should never have offered such a prayer of hope.

I walked toward the nurse's station and recognized Mr. Hutchinson. He was standing there and reading some reports. I was ashamed to talk with him, but he looked up and came toward me.

"Hello, Pastor Ball." He reached out and shook my hand.

"Good morning, Mr. Hutchinson. I promised Steve I'd come back this morning to visit his dad, but. . .I don't know where you've put him."

"Yes, I was watching you in the ICU as you prayed with Ken."

"Yes, I did. But obviously God had other plans. I saw them take him off the ventilator as I was leaving."

"We did. In fact, I think you were in the hall when they moved Mr. Powell from the ICU to the medical ward. He made a dramatic recovery and no longer warranted his ICU bed."

"I—I don't understand." An unexpected warmth flowed through my veins. "A recovery? That's. . .amazing. God is amazing!"

"He certainly is." The surgeon gave me a huge smile.

"So, you're a believer?"

"Yes, I am. As a Christian, my faith makes my work here all the more significant. Come with me. Let me introduce you to the man you prayed for."

We headed down the ward and stopped at a bed near a window. I couldn't comprehend what my eyes were seeing. Yesterday, Ken had bluish-gray, mottled skin with dark circles beneath his eyes. He looked at least eighty years old.

This man was full of color. He had a sparkle in his eyes and had just finished a full English breakfast. He put the morning newspaper down and gave us a warm smile.

I had to look at the name on his chart to believe what I was seeing. "This can't be!" I whispered. "He looks like a different man altogether."

The surgeon moved to Ken's side. "Ken, this is the pastor who prayed for you yesterday."

Ken smiled broadly and reached out to shake my hand. I stood there, stunned. I finally reached out, shook his hand, and didn't want to let go.

His eyes glistened with gratitude. "I'm so grateful to you."

"Oh no, Ken. I really had nothing to do with it. Give your praise to God alone. I was just a warm body reaching out to touch your hand in Jesus' name. He healed your body and restored your life."

Mr. Hutchinson sat on the edge of Ken's bed. "In my capacity as Halton Generals' consultant surgeon, I'm telling you, medically speaking, you should not be alive today. You've been on life support for nearly four days, and your condition was worsening. Yesterday, when Pastor Ball prayed, something happened in your body. From that moment, you began to improve. You're alive because of a miracle through this man's prayer."

All of us were stunned at God's power, but I was shocked. No one but God knew just how empty I was. Just an empty vessel doing what God told me to do. I thought of Jesus performing His first miracle at a wedding in Cana. He simply told the servants to fill the empty vessels with water. The servants had no power. They just obeyed. Jesus took the water and turned it into the best wine. Jesus did this to "reveal[] his glory; and his disciples believed in him" (John 2:11, NIV).

That day, Jesus revealed His glory through Ken's healing.

And what about the apostle Paul? He realized that only in his emptiness could God's power manifest. "But he said to me, 'My grace is sufficient for you, for my power is made perfect in weakness'" (2 Corinthians 12:9, NIV).

Driving home, I felt a calmness in my spirit. God was in charge of my world just as He was in charge of Ken and Steve. My problems hadn't changed, and panic might strike again when another threat hit us. But through it all, my God knew about everything. He would judge the world with righteousness.

Somewhere between my extreme human frailty and God's overwhelming compassion, a rift opened for His power to disrupt natural laws and heal Ken from certain death. God was just and righteous. His purposes were unknown to us, and He simply asked us to trust Him no matter how dark life became.

Steve's faith and hope for his dad's recovery was rewarded. He stayed by his father's side throughout the entire ordeal. As he looked back, he recalled the moment we prayed. His father's recovery was nothing short of a miracle because all medical efforts failed to restore his health. Today, Steve and his wife, Jackie, are active in their church. They love God and acknowledge His almighty power.

Geoff Hutchinson recently said to me, "I believe that experience in the ICU had a profound impact on Ken's life both physically and spiritually." God gave Ken ten more years to mature in his faith, love his family, and be a part of his grandchildren's lives. He is deeply aware that God healed him that day.

Steve recently said to me, "Perhaps my dad's miracle was meant more for you than anyone else."

Maybe so, but Ken and his family enjoyed the immediate blessing of restored life. Yes, God was in charge of all the events of that day in 1988.

My restoration of faith came slowly but was filled with many opportunities to identify with suffering people. I've wept with many people and become their advocate. Because I have seen God's power, I know God is just and holy, and we can trust Him with our lives. "My purpose will stand, and I will do all that I please" (Isaiah 46:10, NIV).

God knew the courts would not give us justice and the guilty man would go free. He knew that day was the culmination of five horrific years of terror for my family. He could have easily caused the judges to enact justice.

But He didn't! He didn't rescue my family from the tormentor. He didn't take away the panic attacks or the depression my wife went through, but He walked with us through each one of those times. "When you pass through the waters, I will be with you. . .When you walk through the fire, you will not be burned; the flames will not set you ablaze" (Isaiah 43:2, NIV).

At such an early age, my sons saw evil, felt its presence, and sensed a hatred one man had toward God that was deep enough to attack even little children. They couldn't understand why the bad things happened, but they watched their parents work through pain while trusting God. As adults, my sons love Jesus supremely, have no doubt in His power, and faithfully raise their own families to love Him.

During one of the scary nights when Mr. Johns frightened the children, we sat together on the upstairs landing and tried to reassure them they were safe. The boys were crying, and Lin and I were weary from the constant attacks. One of the boys asked, "Daddy, why does Mr. Johns hate us so much? What did we do to make him angry?"

"Lads, we have done nothing wrong. You are such good sons and we're proud of you. He hates us because we love Jesus." That was hard for them to understand. "That sort of thing happens in many places around the world. Jesus said, 'If the world hates you, keep in mind that it hated me first'" (John 5:18, NIV). We decided to pray for Mr. Johns and his family in hopes they would find Jesus and turn from their hatred.

Several years after we left the area, a church member notified us that both Noel and his wife died of cancer. No one ever saw any evidence of their salvation, and we were sorry about that. We found no pleasure in their deaths. We know God gives every person a chance to receive Him through repentance. Perhaps in his last days, Mr. Johns remembered our lives and said yes to Him.

As for me, Christ healed my wounded heart and slowly removed my bitterness. Today, wherever I go, God places wounded people in my path, and I walk with them and offer Jesus' hope.

Not long after the court trial, my superintendent said he would do everything possible so that I could take a sabbatical. We'd been in England for fifteen years without a break. A former colleague invited me to take a church position in Denver, Colorado. It was agreed that after one year, we would return to the Frodsham church.

Everyone was happy with that decision, but tragedy struck. My dear brother, mentor, and superintendent, who was only in his early fifties, had a massive heart attack and died. The man who replaced him decided to hire an English pastor to take over the church.

After our sabbatical, we returned to England and were invited to plant a church further north in Lytham St. Annes. Both churches continue to thrive.

We eventually moved to California where we live today. I became a volunteer chaplain for the Los Angeles Sheriff's Department and use my experiences to identify with people in desperate situations, counsel troubled families, counsel suicide victims, and counsel families who have lost a child or a spouse because of crime. I find my greatest joy is knowing that despite everything my children went through, they love God with all their hearts and are raising their children to do the same. The darkness has not been able to extinguish their faith. "The light shines in the darkness, and the darkness has not overcome it" (John 1:5, NIV).

So many of us wonder why God does one thing and not another. Why doesn't He stop the suffering? Ravi Zacharias, a Christian apologist from India, answers it best: "Why don't we wait until we stand before God, face to face, so that we will find that there were reasons why God didn't stop the bullet, so we will see the heinousness of evil and the majesty of God."[1]

Until that glorious day when I see Jesus, I rest in the knowledge that I was privileged to see God's magnificent glory when Jesus healed Ken's broken body. And when I stand before Him, Jesus Himself will wipe every tear from our eyes (Revelation 21:4, NIV).

My God has allowed me to walk through the fire with Him at my side. What glory is this!

Though "When God Heals" is a true story, **Irving H. "Skip" Ball** attributes his storytelling to his evangelistic heart and creative mind. Many of his stories come from real events that occurred while he lived in England. For nearly two decades, he traveled across Europe, living among people who had never heard the gospel. He was in Belfast in Northern Ireland on Bloody Friday when a bomb exploded near his car. Nine people were killed that day. An armed terrorist once pulled him away from preaching to ask, "Is there hope for me?" In France, he confronted demonic strongholds. An East German prisoner once begged him for a Bible.

Skip has written many short stories that display God's miraculous power. His first novel, *Stronghold*, was published in 2007 and

is based on harrowing events that took place in the United Kingdom. His most recent novel, *Bone Boxes*, was published in 2017.

(Endnote)
1 "Atheist Scientist Challenges Christian Apologist Ravi Zacharias," YouTube video, 6:47, posted by "hiskindnessleads leads,"
March 22, 2016, http://youtu.be/OhAxN4pCjp4.

CHAPTER EIGHT

SUPERNATURAL WAR
BILL MYERS

*I have given you authority to trample on snakes
and scorpions and to overcome all the power
of the enemy; nothing will harm you. However,
do not rejoice that the spirits submit to you, but
rejoice that your names are written in heaven.*

—*Luke 10:19–20, NIV*

Santa Monica, California
Sunday Morning

"**D**on't answer it," Brenda said as we headed for our front door.

"But I'm on call," I said. "What if it's important?"

The phone rang again.

She opened the door. "Kenn says he wanted the leaders to start showing up on time."

Of course my wife was right, but I wouldn't let a little thing like that stop me.

The phone rang again.

I looked at Brenda and hesitated. She looked at me and sighed. Then she shut the door and waited.

"It'll just take a minute," I said as I dashed across our tiny apartment. I scooped up the phone in my makeshift office and answered, "Hello?"

The voice on the other end was thin and feeble. "Hello? I was given your number by an answering service. I have been calling various places throughout the morning. Could you tell me what a vine yard is?"

"Oh, you mean *Vineyard*," I said. "Yeah, it's this cool place where people go to hang out and love on Jesus." (It was the 70's, all right? The term "church" was way too establishment).

He cleared his throat. "What exactly do you do?"

"We're like this non-denominational—well, kinda church thing, but we really love Jesus and trust Him to be our savior and cool stuff like that."

There was no reply.

"Hello?"

"When you use the term 'savior,' what do you mean?"

I threw a helpless look to Brenda, who was already setting down her purse with just the right mixture of patience and "I told you so."

As we continued to talk, I learned the man's name was Simon. Carefully, I began to explain to him how God wanted to be our buddy, but our sins were way too outrageous for us to hang out in His presence. (I did mention it was the 70's, right?) I explained why Jesus came, to pay for all our screw-ups so that we wouldn't have to. And all we had to do was ask Him and let Him be our boss. After a few minutes, I finally concluded. "So, what do you think? Pretty awesome, huh?"

"Are you saying He has paid for every immoral action I have ever committed?"

"And ever will. That's right."

"But—I have a past far too heinous to be forgiven."

"No, that's just it. Jesus wasn't just some guy. He is God's only Son. That means He is big enough to pay for everything and for everybody."

"I'm afraid you don't realize the magnitude of my. . ."

"It doesn't matter, man. He's got it covered."

"How is that possible?"

"Because He's God's Son."

"You don't seem to understand."

And around and around we went—Simon telling me his past was too dark to be forgiven, and me insisting Jesus' sacrifice was big enough to pay for everything.

Finally, after twenty or so minutes, I cut to the chase. "Listen, man, it all starts with a prayer. If you're interested, why not give it a shot and just talk to Him. You know, ask Him to forgive you? What have you got to lose?"

I heard a slight groan through the receiver.

"You okay?"

"My head," he muttered. "It's throbbing. It's hurting so bad that I can barely think."

I'd never heard of such a thing happening and reached for what I thought was an obvious explanation. "That's cause it's a big deal. It's like this spiritual struggle. All you have to do is say the prayer. Things will get way better after that, I promise."

But he wouldn't or couldn't believe me. And the more I pressed the issue, the worse his pain grew. "Look," I finally said, "why don't *I* say the words. And if you agree, you can just repeat them after me. How's that sound?"

I was answered by a quiet moan followed by heavy breathing.

"Simon? You okay?"

The breathing grew more labored.

"Simon?"

Then, very faintly, I heard, "Yes. . ."

"Cool."

And so, after reviewing the facts and making sure he understood, I said a brief prayer and Simon repeated my words—confessing he wanted to be forgiven and asking Jesus to be his Lord. I remember the prayer being quick and to the point, and I remember Simon's sincerity.

I also remember his response when we were done.

Silence. When I couldn't stand it any longer, I asked, "So, Simon, how do you feel?"

He took a long, deep breath and blew it out.

"Simon?"

Finally, he said, "This is remarkable. I feel. . ."

I waited.

"I feel. . .wonderful."

I grinned.

"I'm happy." His voice grew stronger. "I *never* feel happy. Forgive me, Mr. Myers, but. . ."

"But what?"

"I have to laugh."

"Well, go ahead," I chuckled. "Don't let me stop you."

When he finished, I wrapped things up. "Listen, it's really important you start reading the Bible, okay? I mean, it's like God's way of talking to His kids. And you've got to start talking to Him. Communication, that's the thing. You can't fall in love with someone if you don't get to know that person. And you don't get to know someone without communicating. He talks to you through His Word. You talk to Him through prayer."

He assured me he would, and we said our goodbyes. I hung up, not only pleased for Simon but also pretty smug about the excuse I would give our pastor, Kenn Gulliksen, when he nailed me for being late.

Little did I realize how quickly that smugness would be thrown out the window.

Santa Monica, California
Saturday Evening

"Hey, Simon, how's it going?"

A week had passed since his first call.

"Fantastic. I'm working on a fascinating paper dealing with prayer and the power of God. That is to say, I am, but I'm not."

"How's that?"

"I hold a pen on a piece of paper. Then I close my eyes and—well, then I lose consciousness."

"You lose consciousness?"

"Yes, partially. My hand starts to move across the page, and I write these remarkable passages, although I have no idea what I've written until I finish and read them."

"Awesome," I said. "Maybe that really does make you like a prophet or something."

"Would you like to hear it?"

"Sure." I glanced at the paper in my $69.95 portable typewriter, grateful I'd found yet another excuse to postpone writing. It was my first contracted book, pretty heady stuff for a twenty-two-year-old. By then I'd already discovered writing wasn't nearly as glamorous as it sounded, especially when your desk is a thin sheet of plywood stretched between two, empty, moving boxes. Actually, the "office furniture" was pretty ingenious, particularly if you're going for the got-no-bucks, newlywed look. But typing could be a problem. The little bounce the plywood gave with every keystroke didn't always work to my advantage. But, thanks to Liquid Paper, I was slowly making progress. Emphasis on the slowly.

So, for the next thirty or forty minutes, Simon read me his paper. Frankly, many of the words and concepts were too lofty for me to understand, though I was struck by his constant use of the phrase, "*The* Christ," and his repeated reference to "letting God rule by deflating our egos." What I did understand, I found to be insightful and spiritual.

When he finally finished, I told him what I thought. I only made one suggestion. "You left out an area."

"Really? And what is that?"

"Worship," I said. "Instead of just talking about prayer and God's power, why not include something about worship?"

"I don't—What do you mean?"

"You know, spending time telling Him how much you love Him and how cool He is? That's part of prayer, too."

"I don't entirely understand."

His answer caught me off guard. Not only had we discussed it during his first call, worship had become such an important part of my life. I was always surprised when others didn't get it. But, knowing he was one week old in the faith and not wanting to embarrass him, I said, "Well, here, let me show you. I'll just start to thank and praise Him over the phone, and when you feel like it, you can join in. How's that sound?"

He agreed and we began. Well, *I* began. He said nothing. I finally stopped and encouraged him to join in. But he remained silent.

"Simon? Are you there?"

Ever so faintly, I heard a quiet groan.

"Simon, what's wrong?"

"Cramps," he moaned. "I have terrible cramps. I must—I have to. . ." The receiver clattered to the floor.

"Simon? Simon!" I waited several moments before he returned. When he spoke, his voice was raw and husky. "I'm sorry."

"What's wrong? What happened?

"I had to vomit."

"Are you sick?"

"I'm okay," he answered. "It's just. . ."

"What?"

"When you were praying, I saw these. . .creatures."

"Creatures?"

"Yes, they were circling me."

"What do you mean, creatures? What did they look like?"

"Some were beautiful, but others—they were awful. Grotesque." I heard him give a little shudder. "One was half animal and half human."

Always the optimist (after all, we had been praying), I asked, "Did they have wings?"

"No. They were frightening. Horrifying."

I thought back to the Bible and remembered how nearly every encounter with a supernatural aspect of God was filled with terror. It seemed everyone's first response to the holy was a face plant on the ground. Until they were told to get up and, "Be not afraid." I figured this put Simon in some pretty good company, so I encouraged him to join with me again.

"No," he said, "you don't understand."

"It's okay," I said. "Telling God how much we love Him is a cool thing. I don't know what's going on, but worshiping Him is good."

Simon was still pretty shook up, and it took several minutes of arguing until he tried again. But I'd no sooner started to pray before the moaning resumed, this time with words. "No," He pleaded. "Please, please. . ."

"It's all right," I said. "Just let yourself go. Just worship God."

"No. . .you don't understand."

"Let go, Simon. Trust Him."

"No, please, please. . ."

Suddenly, his voice was cut off, and I heard a different one. It was still Simon, but his tone was deeper, more confident, and in control. "Hello, Bill. . ."

I gripped the phone a little tighter. "What's happening?" I said. "What's going on?"

The voice continued, "I am an emissary of the Christ."

"What are you talking about? Simon, what's going on?"

"Simon is here, but now I am the one speaking."

"I'm sorry—what?"

"Listen very carefully, for I have come to deliver a message to you from the Christ."

If I said anything, I don't remember. If he said he was an angel, I don't recall. I only remember that for a very long time, he explained in great detail the paper Simon wrote. I also remember Brenda coming in and asking if I wanted to join her and a friend. They were going to The Daisy, a Christian nightclub in Beverly Hills, California, where an acquaintance of ours, Keith Green, was performing.

I shook my head. When she persisted, I covered the mouthpiece and said, "Brenda, please, I'm talking to an angel."

She looked at me kind of funny, but, hey, it was the 70's, and we were new to California. Maybe these sorts of things happened.

The voice continued speaking, but gradually my suspicions rose. They reached their height when the voice said I would instruct and direct Simon as we delivered this great, earth-shaking message to the world. It wasn't so much the words he spoke as the pride I felt rising inside me. I was going to be somebody special. I was going to become someone others would respect and revere. It was a terrific feeling and pretty exciting but not exactly what Jesus had in mind when He called us to meekness and humility.

And with that realization came the first red flag.

Cautious, but still hoping I was hearing a real angel, I began to quietly whisper words of praise to God. The voice never acknowledged what I was doing, and I remember thinking it odd that a holy "emissary of the Christ" would not join in worship. I also remembered a Bible verse that said something like, "Do not believe every spirit, but test the spirits to see whether they are from God."

So, finally, at an appropriate pause, I asked, "Is Jesus Christ your Lord?"

There was a moment's hesitation. And then, very clearly, the voice replied, "Yes, he is my Lord."

I breathed a sigh of relief. He'd passed the test. Still, I couldn't shake my suspicions, particularly as he continued to feed my ego and pride.

Eventually, Simon's voice came back on the line. He sounded like he'd been drugged or was half-asleep. "What happened?" he asked.

I explained as best I could, but in the middle of my explanation, he dropped the receiver a second time and raced away to throw up.

When he returned, I had no idea what to think. Actually, I did. . .but I didn't like what I was coming up with. I was way out of my league but knew that when all else fails, prayer and worship are never bad ideas. So, I asked Simon if he would join me again.

"Why?" he asked. He was leery and exhausted. Who could blame him?

"I don't know," I said. "I'm just not so sure I like what's going on."

After several more minutes of coaxing, I again convinced him. But I'd only prayed a few words before he started to groan, "Please, don't hurt him. Bill's my friend. Don't hurt him. Please, don't. . ."

Suddenly, another voice broke in. It was stronger and far more commanding than the first.

"Hello, William." Before I could answer, it continued, "There is no need to ask because Christ is my Lord. . .and my brother."

Red flag number two. Wasn't claiming to be Christ's brother close to claiming to be His equal?

The second voice repeated much of what the first said about me but in even greater detail. With suspicions continuing to mount, I again dropped into quiet praise and worship. But unlike the first voice, this one stopped and waited until I finished before it continued. We did this—starting and stopping—half a dozen times.

Then came another twist.

"One more thing, William," he said. "You are too hard on yourself. You are human. Like the proverbial coin, you consist of a good side and a bad side. Do not be so demanding of yourself. The bad side is merely part of the same coin. You must learn to embrace both sides."

Red flag number three.

He continued, "I shall give Simon a dream tonight, and you will have the ability to interpret it. That will be the beginning, the first stage of your new partnership." He went on to repeat how great I was and how our teaching would change the world as we spoke of the love of the Christ. Finally, after another long monologue, he ended the talk and Simon resurfaced, once again asking what had happened.

By now I was confused, suspicious, and, like Simon, pretty tired. So, I gave him a quick recap and promised to call him in the morning. In all honesty, I'd be lying if I said I wasn't tempted and moved by all the predictions of my greatness, especially the promises of drawing people closer to God. After all, wasn't that why I'd studied acting and directing at the University of Washington? Wasn't that why I went to film school in Rome? Wasn't that why Brenda and I moved to Los Angeles?

But there were those flags.

I glanced at the clock. It was nearly eleven o'clock in the evening. We'd been on the phone for over four hours. Time flies when you're tempted to sell your soul. I took a deep breath, said another prayer, and reached back for the phone.

It was time to call in the big guns.

"Sorry, pastor, it's Bill Myers. I didn't mean to wake you."

"No," Kenn said, "what's going on?"

I told him everything. When I finished, I waited, hoping for something positive but expecting the worst.

"Bill, when prophets spoke in the Bible, they never lost control of their faculties."

My heart sank. I got the worst.

He continued, "Cramps, throwing up, losing consciousness—that's not how God operates."

"But," I countered, "how can you be so sure?"

"For one, the Scriptures say, 'The spirits of prophets are subject to the control of prophets.'"

"What's that mean?"

"It means that God never invades a person's free will. He will impress prophets on what they should say, but they always have the choice of whether or not to obey Him. And what you're describing—that's anything but free will, isn't it?"

"Yeah, but—well, what about the paper he's writing?"

"It's called automatic handwriting. It's an occult practice. People turn their will over to demons and allow them to use their hands to write."

"But the stuff was so beautiful," I argued. "And it's true. I mean, yeah, some of it's pretty complicated, but it's all true."

"That's another common tactic of Satan. He uses 99 percent truth to get people to swallow his 1 percent lie."

"But I tested the spirits like the Bible says. I asked if Jesus was their Lord."

"You're taking that a bit out of context."

"I am?"

"What was its response?"

"The first one, the weaker one, definitely said Christ was his Lord. And the second one said. . ." I hesitated.

"The second one said what?"

I felt the air being let out of my tires. "He said. . .he was Christ's brother."

"Claiming equality to God. I'd say that pretty well settles it, wouldn't you?"

"Yeah. . .I suppose."

"Praise God."

"Yeah," I replied sarcastically, "praise God."

"No, seriously, *praise God*. You're in way over your head."

"Tell me about it."

"No, that's a good thing. It means you're really going to get the chance to trust Jesus. You'll get to see Him in action and learn."

"Me?" I croaked.

"You bet. Call one of the guys—how 'bout John Smalley? Call John, and you two go over to the man's house and pray with him tomorrow."

"Me?" I repeated. "Isn't this something *you* should be doing?"

"No. You're the one God brought in on this. You're the one He wants to teach.

"You're not serious?"

"Absolutely. This is a terrific learning opportunity for you."

"You're sure I wasn't talking to angels?"

"I'm sure."

"But. . ."

"Good night, Bill."

I sighed, "Good night, pastor," and grudgingly hung up the phone. I don't remember how well I slept, but I'm betting I've had better nights.

Glendale, California
Saturday Evening

Meanwhile, Simon was having his own discussion.

You should never have called, the strongest of the voices inside him said.

"He's just trying to help," Simon said.

You should never have called.

He's right, a second voice agreed, *you should never have called.* No surprise there—the others always agreed with what Simon referred to as the "strongman." They tried never to anger him. Because when the strongman was angry, everyone suffered, including Simon, as evidenced by the cramps and vomiting.

He hadn't always been that way. In fact, the very first day he met Simon, he was just the opposite—gentle, kind, and understanding.

Little seven-year-old Simon cried as he ran through the woods screaming, "Help me! Somebody, please?" It was late autumn in Pennsylvania. A thin band of smoke hung in the air, sharp and sweet-smelling, from neighbors burning leaves. And it was cold. Bitterly cold.

"Boy!" He heard his father shouting from the porch. But Simon could not return. Not when the man was like this. Granted, he had no coat, only a t-shirt, and he shivered fiercely. But the welts covering his little body were clear indications that he could not go back.

He stumbled through the undergrowth crying, "Help me! Help me!" But no one answered. At least no one he saw.

Do you want help?

The voice was so clear and present that Simon looked over his shoulder to see who was behind him. No one was there.

Are you certain you want help? It was tender and compassionate. Not at all like his dad's.

"Boy!" He heard his father stumbling down the steps. "I swear to God, if you don't get your ragged butt back here. . ."

Do you want my help? The voice repeated.

"Yes!"

"Boy! Where are you?"

"Yes, please. . .please, help me."

Then do exactly as I say. The voice gave careful instructions, directing Simon through the woods until he arrived at a small cabin. It was well kept and recently painted but definitely showing its age.

"Here?" Simon asked.

Knock on the door.

"But. . ."

She's expecting you.

"But I don't know who she is," he whined.

The voice did not answer.

"Hello?"

There was only silence.

"Hello? Are you still here?"

Again, no answer.

He was shivering hard, clouds of steam rising from his mouth. "I don't know who she is. I don't know who she is." But no amount of complaining produced a response. Finally, mustering all of his courage, he raised his hand and knocked on the wooden planks of the door.

Moments later, a thin, older woman with neatly brushed, gray hair appeared. "Well, hello there."

He stood, shivering, unsure of what to say.

"Dear me." She opened the door wider. "You must be freezing."

He hesitated then stepped inside. The warmth of the room wrapped around him. The only light came from a stone fireplace that hissed and popped from across the room. The place smelled a little dank, like the forest on a hot, humid day.

She closed the door and quickly crossed to some cabinets. "Here, let me get you a blanket. Poor thing," she said as she pulled one from a pile. "I can't believe anyone would let you outside dressed like that. Please," she said and motioned to the rocker by the fireplace, "come sit. Please."

And so began their friendship.

The woman, he called her Aunt Lily, was a student of mind control and the power of thought. He had no idea what that meant, but he was an eager and willing learner. Until her death in his mid-teens, she was able to teach him much. And what she couldn't teach, the "spirit guides" she introduced him to could.

"I didn't mean to make you angry," Simon told the strongman as he pulled back the covers and slipped into bed.

I will repair the damage.

The words left him unsettled. "And Bill," he said. "You won't harm Bill?"

On the contrary, William will soon be our ally.

Glendale, California
Sunday Afternoon

John looked over to me and asked, "You ready?"

I took a deep breath. We drove the forty-five minutes from Santa Monica to Glendale, listening to and singing along with some worship tapes. (It should have been thirty minutes, but, as usual, I got us lost.) We parked one block away from Simon's house where we had spent the last ten minutes praying—asking for God's wisdom, for His protection, and, due to Simon's recent, open-heart surgery, that Simon would be strong enough to survive whatever happened. We also spent time confessing our sins to each other and to God. If we really were dealing with demons, and if they really could see stuff normal folks couldn't, I didn't need the embarrassment of them bringing up any hidden baggage.

"Okay," I took another breath. "Let's do it."

We opened the doors of my little Datsun (little because I'm six foot two and John was six foot four) and stepped out into the afternoon light.

It had already been a long day.

Earlier that morning, I had called Simon and told him I was afraid that I was wrong. As gently as possible, I explained that those voices probably weren't angels but. . .demons. Obviously, that wasn't well-received, and we had another long discussion until he finally agreed to let me come over.

And now, here we were, at his door. I knocked. There was no answer.

I was about to knock again when the door slowly opened.

And there, before me, stood a small, pudgy man in his late forties who wore glasses. I was struck by how young he looked compared to how old his voice sounded.

"Bill?" he asked.

"Hi, Simon." And then, before I could stop myself, I reached out and hugged him. I'm not sure why. Maybe it was because of all the time we'd put in together on the phone. Or because he had been through so much. Whatever the reason, I held him tight, feeling a real love and compassion. Though he didn't return the embrace, he quietly endured it. Only later, after everything was finished, did he tell me it was the hug that did it. He said that from the moment he felt that love, he knew everything would work out.

John and I sat on the small sofa in the front room. Simon was in his easy chair near the picture window.

"What if it doesn't work?" he repeated.

"It will work," I said.

"But what if you're wrong? What if they really are from God?"

It was old, familiar territory—questions we'd been through a dozen times on the phone. But, remembering how we had broken the cycle before, I said, "Okay, if you don't mind, let's try this. If they're really from God, let's just sit back and worship Him. I mean, if they're really angels, they won't mind, will they?"

Simon pushed up his glasses. "No. . .I suppose that would be all right."

And so we began to pray. Nothing fancy. We just closed our eyes and started thanking God for His goodness. But no more than ten seconds passed before Simon's head began rolling from side to side. "No. . ." he whispered. "Please, no, no. . ."

"Simon?" I asked. "Are you okay?"

A low, guttural growl came from deep inside his chest as he began to squirm then twist.

John and I traded looks and immediately crossed the room to him. Fearing he might hurt himself, we dropped to our knees and held him down. (I suppose if we had had more faith, we would have just sat comfortably on the couch. But we were definitely new to all this.) Suddenly, his eyes popped open, and he glared at me with bone-chilling hatred while letting loose lots of cursing. His entire body began to writhe and convulse. Despite John's size and my size, it was all we could do to hold the little man down. And because of his recent heart operation, I kept thinking, *Wonderful, how am I going to tell Mom and Dad I've been convicted of murder while casting out demons?*

The swearing grew louder, and we amped up our own volume of praise. It was time. We were about to practice what we had read in the Scriptures. I forget who was first, but either John or I shouted, perhaps a bit too dramatically, "In the name of Jesus Christ of Nazareth, come out of him!"

Simon immediately stiffened. He threw back his head, screamed an oath, then suddenly went limp.

"Simon?" I threw a glance to John. "Simon, are you there?"

Slowly he opened his eyes. He blinked once or twice before focusing on us.

"Are you okay?" I asked.

"Yes," he answered hoarsely. It was his own voice.

"Where did it go?" John asked.

Simon paused, as if listening, then he shook his head. "I don't know, but he's not here anymore."

I relaxed a bit. This was easier than I thought. And then, with a writer's curiosity, I asked, "What was it like? What happened?"

Simon shook his head. "He sure hated that name."

"You mean 'Jesus'?" I asked.

"Not just 'Jesus.' Several people have that name. But when you added 'Christ' to it, everything turned chaotic." He paused. "It felt as if I was being held down deep inside myself. But whenever I called out Christ's name, I was allowed to surface." He glanced up to me. "And you two—whenever you spoke using His name. . .well, you saw what happened." Again he shook his head, quietly marveling. "You have no idea who you are. No idea at all."

"What do you mean?" I asked.

"They're scared to death of you."

It was supposed to be good news, but I exhaled slowly and repeated, "*They?*"

Simon nodded.

"There's more than one?" John asked.

Simon's eyes fluttered. His face twitched then contorted. Suddenly, his entire body convulsed. Still on our knees, John and I grabbed his arms again and pinned them down on the chair. The eyes exploded open, filled with the same rage as before. But when he spoke, it was with a different, higher voice.

"You can't send me away," it said. "He wants to keep me."

"That's not true," I answered. "He just told us. . ."

"You are nothing!" The eyes shot to me and the voice sneered. "You have no authority."

I shook my head. "You're wrong. You saw what just happened. We have plenty of authority."

"Liar."

"You're the liar." I was getting hot under the collar. "Satan is the author of lies. That's all you know how to do. Just last night you told me. . ."

John interrupted, "Bill."

". . .you were some sort of emissary."

"I am."

"No, you're not."

"Bill!"

I looked over to John.

"Don't debate? That's what it wants: to sidetrack us so that we take our eyes off Jesus."

Simon turned toward John and hissed. "You think you're so clever. Well, you're nothing. You have no. . ."

"You take that up with Jesus Christ," John said, "not us."

"Do you honestly believe that. . ."

"Talk to Jesus, not me."

"That's right," I said, having caught on. "Jesus is the one who gave us the authority. You take that up with Him."

Simon spun around to me and spat in my face. He was a pretty good shot. But instead of getting angry, I broke out laughing. If this was the best he had, bring it on.

"What's your name, demon?" John said.

Simon turned back to him. "You are so incredibly ugly."

"What is your name?"

"You know nothing of real beauty."

"Your name," John repeated. "What's your name?"

"My name. . ." Simon raised his chin slightly. "My name is. . .Vanity."

"Then, Vanity, by the power and authority of Jesus Christ, I order you to come out of Simon."

"He wants me. I don't have to leave if. . ."

"Come out of him," I said.

It turned back to me "You have no. . ."

"Now," John ordered. "By the power and authority of Jesus Christ, we order you out of him, now."

"You are so incredibly ugly. If you only knew. . ."

"Now."

And so we continued—the thing trying to engage us in a debate, and John and me sticking to our guns—until, finally, Simon tensed, screamed, and slumped into his chair.

I sat back on my heels, catching my breath. When Simon surfaced and turned to me, I asked, "Why was that one so much harder?"

He glanced away and shrugged.

"Is it true?" John asked. "Did you really want to keep him?"

At first Simon gave no answer. But we continued to press him until, finally, he nodded and answered a bit sheepishly, "Yes."

"Is that it?" John asked. "Are there any more?"

"I can't tell for certain. I think two or maybe three more. They're hiding behind each other, so I can't see."

I nodded, wiping the spit off my face.

Obviously embarrassed, he said, "I'm so terribly sorry."

"Don't worry." I grinned. "I wash."

"You ready to try some more?" John asked.

Simon nodded, dabbed the sweat from his face, and we began.

After several minutes, another one came out after the same tensing of the body, the same screaming, and the same Simon going limp. And then another. And another. Each one taking a little longer than the last. Each one swearing, writhing, and using me for spit target practice. After each was expelled, Simon surfaced, and we'd take a break to talk. That's when he told us how the first spirit, the strongman, entered him at the old lady's cabin. And how, gradually, one by one, the others joined the cluster.

"But you were just a little boy," I said.

"It was still my choice. I was the one who made the decision. And they were true to their word; they did give me power."

"What about your parents?" John asked. "How did they handle it?"

"My father was not at home much. And my mother, she was a devout Christian."

"Did she know what was going on?" I asked.

He nodded. "She would warn the others to stay away from me. And when I frightened or hurt them, she took me upstairs to explain why what I did was wrong."

"How did you respond?"

"I'd scream and threaten, often throwing a fit. But she never gave up. She was always there—instructing me, guiding me as best she knew how."

"So, she was teaching you right from wrong in spite of them."

"Yes." His voice grew softer. "And the day she died—it was right after my eighteenth birthday—she used all her strength to come downstairs to the basement where I was stoking the furnace, and she said. . ." He took an uneven breath. "She said God spoke to her and promised to answer her prayers. She said He promised my life would be hard, but before I died, I would become a Christian."

John and I looked on quietly.

"It took thirty-eight years. . ." Simon swallowed and continued. "But, here we are, just as she said."

The three of us sat in silence, each of us, no doubt, considering the power of a mother's prayers. Prayers answered long after the grave.

I glanced at my watch. It was nearly five o'clock in the evening. By our count, at least six different spirits had come out of Simon. I asked, "How many more of them do you think there are?"

He shook his head. "I'm not certain. But, please, there is no need to worry so much about my heart."

I looked at him in surprise. "You read my mind?"

"No, that's one thing they can't do, at least with Christians. And one reason they hate you so much. But they are experts at observing and analyzing. They look for tiny, barely discernable behavior traits to discover what you are really thinking. And. . ." he smiled gently, "they know you are concerned for my health."

I nodded. Guilty as charged.

"But there is something else you should know as well."

I looked on, waiting.

"In the back bedroom, there are sketches. Sketches I've been making of you."

I felt the hair on my neck rise. "That's pretty freaky," I said. "You've never seen me until today."

"I know. But I knew you'd be the one to help."

"Since last week?" I asked. "You've been sketching me since last week?"

He shook his head. "No. Since you were a little boy."

It was difficult to keep track, but by the early evening, we'd removed another two or three of the things. For whatever reason, each seemed a little more difficult to remove and took longer than the previous one. In every case, John called it up to the surface in Jesus' name and demanded to know its identity. Neither of us was sure if this was necessary, but we remembered Christ doing it with the demoniac in Luke 8, so we figured it wasn't a bad example to follow.

The oddest was the one that called itself Lust. As soon as we brought it to the surface, it started coming on to us, rubbing our hands and speaking with a lisp so affected it was almost comical. What was not comical was how it continued to remain. No matter what we said or did, it would not go.

"Oh, I'm never leaving him, handsome," it said, doing its best to flirt with me. "He wants me. He thinks I'm love."

I realized how sad and true that must be for so many people. And I realized something else as well. "Simon," I said. "Let Simon come up. I want to speak to Simon."

"Oh, Simon won't be able to. . ."

"In the name of Jesus Christ, I demand to speak to Simon."

After a moment or two of resistance, the spirit fell back and Simon surfaced, gasping and calling upon Jesus as he always did. When he was finally in control, I said, "This one is harder than all the others. Is it because you want to hang on to it like you did with that vanity one?"

"No, why would you say. . ."

"Simon, be honest. Is the reason this one won't leave because you want to keep it more than the others?"

He glanced away, refusing to look me in the eyes, and I had my answer. It wasn't something John and I were doing wrong. And it wasn't for lack of power on Jesus' part. As before, it all had to do with what Simon wanted, what he *really* wanted. Just as Kenn had said, it was all about free will.

After several minutes of convincing Simon that love was much deeper than lust, that lust was just Satan's twisting of God's deeper gift of intimacy, we began again. Still, Simon's words, which claimed he wanted to be rid of the spirit, were much different than his will. And it took nearly an hour of our ordering it to leave and of Simon's squirming and thrashing before it was finally expelled.

By now the day was growing late and we were all exhausted. Hoping we were done, we began wrapping up with a little more worship and prayer. . .until Simon began rolling his head back and forth, again begging the spirits not to hurt me. Suddenly, he stopped, opened his eyes, and glared.

"What's your name?" John demanded.

The voice was deep and authoritative, like the one I'd first heard over the phone. "My name. . .is Simon."

"That's not true," I said. "What's your real name?"

Its eyes shifted to me. "I told you, William, my name is Simon."

I threw a look to John. This didn't make sense.

John repeated, "We order you to tell us your name."

"I am the spirit of intellect. I have more intelligence than the three of you combined."

Remembering not to argue and to put our focus on Christ, I agreed. "Yeah, probably, but you're no match for Jesus. Now, what's your name?"

It ignored me. "I am the reason the LAPD contacted Simon to find missing bodies. I am the reason celebrities seek his counsel. Did he tell you about Katharine Hepburn?"

"What's your name?"

"I have told you. My name is Simon."

"You're lying," I said.

It turned to me and smiled. "I have been with him since the beginning. His personality is so mingled with mine that he has no idea where I begin and where he leaves off. He has no idea who he is. He cannot exist without me."

Unsure of what to do, we returned to worshipping. After several minutes, Simon fought his way back to the surface.

"Is it true?" I asked. "Is this the first one, the one you called the strongman?"

"Yes," Simon said, "he's. . ." Suddenly, he winced.

"Are you okay?"

He nodded and gasped, "He's the one." He took another breath, fighting to continue. "He ducked behind the others—shoving them forward for protection."

"So, it's the last?" John asked.

"Yes." He winced again, his face contorting in pain. "It's just this one. Is it possible to allow him to remain?"

John and I both fidgeted. Like I said, we were pretty tired.

Simon persisted. "Please, it is just one."

John finally shook his head. "No. If you keep him, he could invite the others back, just like he did before."

"No," Simon argued. "He promises he won't."

"Simon," I said, "you can't trust him. You know that."

And so began another long, circular debate—Simon wanting to keep the final spirit, the one that had been his companion for over forty years, and John and me trying to convince him that he needed to be completely free. Eventually we prevailed and Simon finally agreed, giving us permission to continue.

This one, this strongman, was the most difficult of all to expel. And it took the longest. When it wasn't pointing out our weaknesses, it was insisting that Simon would be a vegetable without its presence. We refused to believe it, but Simon wasn't so sure. As a result, the struggle lasted well beyond the first hour and dragged into a second.

And then, as we approached nine o'clock in the evening, the breakthrough suddenly happened. Like so many times before, we were commanding the spirit to leave, and finally, finally Simon threw back his head and screamed. It wasn't quite like the other screams. This one was a bit stiffer and more reserved, but it was a scream. And as it faded, Simon's body relaxed until he eventually opened his eyes.

"Was that it?" I asked. "Are we done?"

"Yes." Simon took a deep breath and blew it out. "Yes."

"They're gone?" John repeated. "All of them?"

Simon nodded. "Yes. There's just the one in white who. . ." He stopped then resumed nodding. "Yes, they have all left."

Too exhausted to question Simon any further and wanting to believe him, John and I rose stiffly to our feet. After a round of hugs, we promised to stay in touch, and I encouraged Simon to find a church. If not ours, then somewhere else. It had been a long, long day, but we had succeeded. We were as victorious as Jesus promised His disciples they would be.

Unfortunately, like His disciples, we didn't always get things right.

Santa Monica, California
Monday Evening

"So, you're feeling pretty good?" I asked.

"I feel wonderful," Simon exclaimed.

"That's terrific." I looked across the room, watching Brenda. She was excited. Although money was tight, we were preparing to go out for dinner.

I directed my attention back to the phone. "So, what have you been doing all day?"

"Mostly resting."

"I hear that," I chuckled. "We really ran you through the wringer. Are you getting a chance to read the Bible?"

"Not yet. But I am writing some more."

I paused. "Simon. . ."

"No, no, this time it is in my own handwriting. I am completely awake and cognizant."

"And it's in your own words?"

He hesitated.

"Simon. . .is the writing in your own words?"

His answer came softly. "No."

I felt the joy of last night drain away.

He quickly explained, "But the topic is extremely reverent, and it gives glory to the Christ."

"But you're telling me it's not your own words."

Brenda heard the tone of my voice. I tried to smile. But she saw through it, and I watched her wilt ever so slightly.

Simon continued, "I have not felt this good in a very long time."

"Simon. . ."

"As a matter of fact, I'm boarding a flight to New York in a few hours. I plan to tell all of my friends about this remarkable event and. . ."

I cut him off as gently as possible. "Simon. . .there's still one left, isn't there?" I glanced back to Brenda as she turned and walked to the kitchen.

"Everything is good."

"But the words aren't yours."

"Well, no. But perhaps. . ." His voice trailed off.

"Perhaps what?"

"Perhaps this one really is an angel."

"Simon."

"He is good. I'm certain of it."

Unsure of what to say, I returned to the old standby. "If that's so, let's spend a couple of minutes worshipping together."

"I really don't see a need. . ."

"Okay?"

He paused then said, "Absolutely, I see no reason why not."

"Great. I'll start off and you jump in whenever you want."

He agreed and we began. But I'd barely said a word before the commanding voice, the one Simon called the strongman, surfaced. I sighed. Had we worked so long and so hard just to be back where we started?

"Who are you?" I demanded.

"I told you," the voice said. "I am Simon."

It made no sense. Demons are supposed to obey believers. So how could this one keep lying and dodging my command? And he wasn't through.

"He spoke correctly when he told you that we are going to New York," it said. "He is mine. I am taking him to New York, and you will never see him again."

"No." I rose to my feet. "You can't do that."

"I can do anything I want. You have no authority over me."

"That's not true."

"Of course it is. Open your eyes, you ignorant (insert his usual expletives here)."

"What's your name?" I demanded. "By the authority of Jesus Christ, I order you to tell me your name."

"I told you."

"Your name. What is your name?"

"Simon. My name is Simon."

"That's not true. I want to speak to Simon. I order you to release Simon and. . ."

"I am Simon!"

I scowled. If the Bible was true and I had authority over this thing, then something else was wrong. I kept pursuing. "I command you to release Simon and let me speak to him. Now!"

Simon began to gasp as he often did when surfacing. "Jesus, Jesus. . ."

"Simon." I began to pace. "Simon, talk to me."

"I AM SIMON!"

For whatever reason, Simon slipped back under, and we had to go through the whole process again—my worshipping, the strongman swearing, and Simon struggling to fight back to the surface. That's when it dawned on me. Maybe the thing really *was* telling the truth. Maybe it really was obeying me, and its name really was Simon. And if its name was Simon, then. . .

Another thought came to mind. "Simon!" I called. "Simon, what's on your birth certificate?"

He surfaced but only for a moment.

"What's the name on your birth certificate? Do you have another name? What's your—"

And then I heard him in a faint whisper. "Sam. . ."

"Did you say, 'Sam'?" I practically shouted.

"Yes. . ." His voice disappeared and was replaced by the strongman. Only this time the thing was screaming, literally shrieking and swearing, so loud that Brenda could hear it across the room.

I gave my usual response—whispered praise.

"I'M HANGING UP NOW!" It shouted.

"No," I said, feeling a surge of authority. "I forbid it."

"YOU HAVE NO—"

"You cannot hang up."

"I'M HANGING UP AND I'M TAKING HIM TO NEW YORK."

"No."

"I'M TAKING HIM TO NEW YORK AND THERE'S NOTHING—"

"No! I forbid it!"

Despite its screams and threats, the thing could not hang up, which gave me a moment to think of a plan. I'd call John, and we'd race back to Simon's (i.e., Sam's) in hopes of getting there before he left.

The thing continued shrieking and swearing.

Then again, if I had the authority to prevent it from hanging up, didn't I also have the authority to delay its leaving until we got there? I looked over to Brenda, who was setting a pan of water on the stove to boil. And if I could delay it a little, couldn't I delay it a lot? I watched as she pulled a box of mac and cheese from the cupboard. Couldn't I order it to stay at the house until after I had taken my wife to dinner?

"YOU HAVE NO AUTHORITY! I AM TAKING HIM TO NEW YORK AND YOU HAVE NO AUTH—"

"No!" I shouted.

"I AM HANGING UP!"

"In the name of Jesus Christ, I order you to shut up!"

It fell silent.

I was on a roll and continued. "Sam will not be able to leave his house until—" I paused and then went for broke, "—until 10:30 tomorrow morning."

"YOU HAVE NO AUTHORI—"

"Sam cannot leave until 10:30 a.m. tomorrow!"

"I'M HANGING UP NOW!"

"No, I forbid it!"

But even as I gave the order, I remembered thinking, *Man, I'm tired of this. I've done everything I can. It really wouldn't be so bad if he hung up now and—*

And, just like that, the line went dead.

"Hello?" I said. "Hello?"

He'd hung up. I don't know if the spirit had heard the tone in my voice or what. But it knew the words of my mouth did not line up with the convictions of my heart. Still, I wasn't worried because I had meant every word about it not leaving until 10:30 tomorrow morning.

And with that strange yet absolute assurance, I turned back to Brenda. "What are you doing?" I asked.

"Fixing dinner," she said.

"I thought we were going out."

She turned to me and saw the smile on my face. Without a word, she turned off the stove and crossed to the bedroom to grab her coat. We were going out for barbecued ribs, her favorite.

Glendale, California
Tuesday Morning

It was 10:15 a.m. when John and I, along with Brent Rue, another pastor friend, turned the corner onto Sam's street. Of all the drama John and I had experienced, I found these next few minutes revealed the most about a believer's authority in Christ.

"There he is," I said, pointing. Sam was outside on his front lawn, pacing back and forth.

Brent pulled the car up to the curb, and I climbed out. "Hey there. . .Sam."

His face was full of fear and confusion.

I tried to sound casual. "So, man, what's happening?"

"I can't, I can't step off the property; it's not 10:30." He blinked and pushed up his glasses. "Unless I have permission, I can't leave."

"Permission from who?"

He looked up to me. "You?"

I nodded. "Here, take my arm, and let's go for a walk." He took my arm, and we stepped off his lawn and onto the sidewalk. He looked down, amazed. So was I.

A few minutes later, Brent suggested we go to the church offices, and we all agreed.

Sherman Oaks, California
Tuesday Afternoon

In many ways, the next few hours were the same ol' same ol' as we called up and cast out another three of four spirits. Although there were a few interesting highlights, some even comical. My favorite was when Kenn, who was next door on the phone, kept covering the receiver to block out the screaming and swearing. Then there was our friend, soon-to-be recording artist Keith Green, who dropped by. Keith loved a good fight. He particularly enjoyed seeing Simon surface so that he could taunt him about spending eternity in hell.

We'd been going at it for nearly four hours with only a few successes. We tried everything—worship, giving commands, checking to make sure Sam was in agreement, and prayer (lots of prayer). But, the fact of the matter is that we had run out of material. After all those hours, it felt like we were simply repeating ourselves. Everyone was growing frustrated and exhausted. And then, for reasons I'll never understand other than acting "on a whim," I began to recite the Lord's Prayer.

That's when Simon went ballistic. It was as if we had poured acid on him the way he writhed and cursed and screamed. At first we thought it was the prayer itself. But, still having that writer's curiosity, I did a little experiment and recited some other passage from the Bible. The results were just as dramatic. Only later did we recall how among all the weapons listed for battle in Ephesians

6:17, there was only one given to us to use for offense: "the sword of the Spirit, which is the word of God" (NIV).

We remembered how when Jesus was tempted by Satan in the wilderness, the Lord fought back with only one thing—the Word of God. Interesting He did not use guns or rockets or go nuclear. Instead the Creator of the universe fought the most evil force in the universe with what they both considered to be the most powerful weapon in the universe—God's Word. The same Word Hebrews 4:12 says is "Sharper than any double-edged sword" (NIV).

Finding this new weapon in our arsenal excited and renewed our energy. We read from all sorts of places in the Bible, though for the record, Psalm 121 was our Scripture of choice. And, whenever one of the spirits irritated me or I just wanted to spice things up a bit, I'd open the Bible and read.

Was I being immature? Sometimes. Was it fun? Definitely. I even enjoyed it when Simon surfaced, looked me straight in the eyes, and snarled, "You (insert usual expletives here), you are the one responsible for all of this. I will kill you." But instead of my first response, which had been dry-mouthed fear, I actually considered its hatred a compliment. And to show my appreciation, I simply flipped to another section of Scripture and began to read. Granted, there was more than the usual amount of spit flying. And when Simon managed to free a leg, I received a powerful kick to the gut. But the satisfaction it provided was well worth the price of admission.

As with the earlier encounter, I'm sure we made lots of mistakes. To this day, I don't know why we thought it was important to know each spirit's name. And I still think, had we enough faith, we might not have had to hold him down. But we kept muddling forward and slowly but surely made progress.

Nevertheless, as 6:00 p.m. rolled around, I was beat—emotionally and physically.

"I've got to take a break," I said.

Suddenly, Sam surfaced and cried out, "No! Don't leave me, Bill. There's only one left! There's only Simon. He's the only—"

"Shut up, Samuel!" the other voice shouted.

But Sam would not be silenced. When he went under, it took only a few seconds before he was back up and yelling, "He has no one to hide behind! He's all by himself. He's—"

"SHUT UP!" Simon turned to me and shouted. "I'm going to kill him! I'm going to throw him out that window!"

Could we have stopped him with a simple, verbal command? Probably. But no one was taking chances. I joined John, Brent, and whoever else was in the room, and we held him tight. We prayed, worshipped, and gave commands as Sam kept fighting back to the surface, shouting, "He's the only one left!"

"SHUT UP! I WILL KILL—"

"He's the only one left! He's—"

"SHUT UP! SHUT UP! SHUT—"

And suddenly, amidst the screaming, fighting, and praying, Sam's body went completely limp.

The room grew deathly silent.

"What happened?" I asked.

"Sam?" John said. "Sam, can you hear me?"

"Is he alive?" I asked. "Check his breathing."

John put his hand on Sam's chest. "He's breathing. His heart's going a mile a minute, but he's alive."

I turned to Brent. His face was filled with amazement.

"What's wrong?" I asked.

"I just saw. . ." Brent took a breath. "I just saw Jesus."

"You what?" I said.

"It was only for a second, but, yeah, I saw Jesus."

"What'd He do? Did He say anything?" John asked.

"No, He just sat there. And He just—when Simon was doing all the screaming, He just looked at him."

"And?"

"And Simon left."

"Just like that?" John asked.

Brent nodded. "Yeah. Jesus just gave him this glance, and the thing split. He didn't even have time to scream."

Everyone fell silent. Was that it then? Were we finished? No special effects? No big climax? Not even some eerie, echoing scream?

Apparently so. It had nothing to do with our shouting or its screaming or any other type of drama. Instead it had everything to do with Jesus simply showing up and exercising His authority. We were amazed. Literally awestruck.

I don't remember much after that. Just us sitting in quiet wonder at the power displayed with so little effort. A simple glance. That was all it took. For the briefest moment, the glory of Jesus Christ appeared, and, suddenly, everything was made right.

"Bill, do you know what it's like to feel the wind on your face?"

I glanced at my watch, fearing I was entering into another one of Sam's marathon calls. "Oh yeah," I said. "We live near the beach, so a breeze is always—"

"No, no. I mean to *really* feel it."

I sighed quietly. "No. Tell me, Sam, what does it feel like?"

So began another one of our long conversations. Sometimes we'd talk over the phone, sometimes over a meal. A couple of times, Brenda and I picked him up and brought him over to the apartment.

"And insects. Bill, have you ever stopped to examine insects? What remarkable creatures!"

Talking to Sam was like talking to someone who'd just stepped out of years of solitary confinement. It was as if for the first time in forty years, he was able to fully see, touch, and experience the life all around him. When he wasn't marveling over the beauty of creation, he was marveling over the love of its Creator. And he couldn't wait to tell everybody he knew.

One evening, we were eating dinner at Jerri's Famous Deli. I was just about to dig into my favorite, ultra-thick pastrami on rye, when he said, "I spoke with the students taking my extension class on mind control last night."

"What did you say?" I asked, biting into the sandwich.

"I explained that much of what I taught them was wrong."

I nodded, continuing to chew.

"I told them it was a satanic trick that demons use to try and control people."

"How'd that go?" I said, my mouth full of food.

"A lot better than when I told them they must each receive Jesus Christ as their personal Lord and Savior."

I coughed, nearly choking.

"And next week I will be appearing on the local psychic show."

I swallowed.

"I'm their favorite guest. I can hardly wait to tell them about Jesus Christ."

I nodded, wondering if his popularity with them was about to end. Then, as tactfully as possible, I said, "You know, Sam. You might want to take things just a little slower."

"What do you mean?"

"I mean, let people warm up to you a little first."

"Why?"

"So that they don't think you're some crazy person or something."

"I disagree." He frowned then shook his head. "If a person is drowning, does he need to trust the only one willing to throw him a rope?"

I started to answer but was too slow.

"Actually, in my opinion, you are being far too timid."

"*Me?*"

"Yes, you. What you have to tell people is the most important truth in the world."

"Right. . ."

"So, why don't you tell them?"

"I try."

"Not enough. You pussyfoot around, exclaiming how *cool* and *groovy* Jesus is."

"You have to gain a person's trust so that they don't think you're just using them."

"Using them?" His voice grew louder. "How is saving somebody's soul from the fiery pit of hell using them?"

I glanced self-consciously at those sitting nearby. When I looked back, Sam was shaking his head. I took another bite of the sandwich. It wasn't quite as tasty as I remembered.

He spoke again. This time his voice was a little softer and just a little sad. "You simply have no idea who you are, do you?"

"You've said that before. What's that supposed to mean?"

He gave his head another shake and quietly repeated, "You have no idea."

Several days later, we had another discussion. It was outdoors. I'm not certain, but it might have been on the beach during one of our Sunday services. (Back then, you could perceive the depth of someone's commitment by the amount of sand in their Bible.)

"I haven't had the chance to tell you what happened yesterday," he said. "I was visiting a friend, a demon-possessed friend and—"

"Wait," I interrupted. "You visited a demoniac. . .by yourself?"

"Of course."

"You should have had one of us go with you. You should have called me so that I could have at least been praying. What happened?"

"Actually, it was fairly anticlimactic."

"Anticlimactic?"

He nodded. "I simply called the demons to the surface and said, 'I know who you are and what you want. And in the name of Jesus Christ, come out of him.'"

"And?"

He shrugged. "And they came out. It took fifteen minutes." Seeing my jaw slacken, he replied, "Honestly, I don't know why you made such a big production over it."

I could only shake my head, marveling. Maybe we had underestimated our authority. Maybe Jesus Christ really is that powerful.

And to this day, I'm still reminded of his earlier comment: "You just don't know who you are." It seems the devil's greatest feat is not spreading his darkness throughout the world, it's keeping believers' identities in Christ a secret, especially from themselves. His greatest accomplishment is convincing us to believe his accusations that we are weak, wretched sinners—just lucky to be saved— instead of trusting that Christ is great enough to *fully* pay for *all* our failures on the cross.

Over and over, I've seen myself paralyzed by the accuser's voice, tied up by my own inadequacies, believing Christ's sacrifice just wasn't good enough. I believe it's time to get over ourselves. It's time to get on the other side of the cross and employ His earth-changing weapons of prayer, praise, and the Word to destroy the enemy's darkness, whatever form it may take.

Bill Myers is a bestselling author and an award-winning producer whose work has won over eighty national and international awards, including the C. S. Lewis Honor Award. His children's works include the *McGee and Me!* television show and the *The Incredible Worlds of Wally McDoogle* book series. His best known book for adults is *Eli*, a retelling of the Gospel as if it happened today. When he's not writing books, he's managing his production company, Amaris Media International. For more information, visit www.BillMyers.com.

For a more detailed version of this account, please check out the Kindle edition of *Supernatural War* on Amazon.

To find out more about these and other miraculous stories, please visit www.WhenGodHappens.com for the following: exclusive video interviews with the storytellers, premium content, free stories, the ongoing God Stories blog, and the opportunity to share your miracle story.